PICKER'S
POCKET·GUIDE

BASEBALL
MEMORABILIA

How to Pick Antiques like a Pro

718669892

JEFF FIGLER

JAN 0 7 2015

Published by

Krause Publications, a division of F+W,
A Content + eCommerce Company
700 East State Street • Iola, WI 54990-0001
715-445-2214 • 888-457-2873
www.krausebooks.com

To order books or other products call toll-free 1-800-258-0929
or visit us online at www.krausebooks.com

Pictured on the cover: Circa 1990 Mickey Mantle "No. 7" signed fielder's glove, **$2,031.50**; Babe Ruth-signed baseball (see P. 83); the 1947 Ted Williams Triple Crown season game-used vault marked bat, one of the finest Williams' game-used bats known to the hobby, **$77,675**; St. Louis Cardinals mascot bobbing head doll (see P. 118); Honus Wagner baseball card (see pages 57-59); Hank Aaron baseball card (see P. 64); and Derek Jeter's jersey (see P. 106). *All photos courtesy of Heritage Auctions.*

ISBN-13: 978-1-4402-4278-6
ISBN-10: 1-4402-4278-X

Designed by: Jana Tappa
Edited by: Kristine Manty

Printed in China

To Nathan, a father's dream.

CONTENTS

Introduction

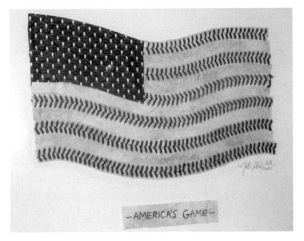

An American flag made out of old baseballs symbolizes that the sport is our national pasttime.

Jeff Figler

I'm obsessed with collecting. That's why I've written books about my passion and established a non-profit museum devoted, in large part, to sports collectibles—and to raising money that benefits children's charities. With this book, I hope to make sports collecting, specifically collecting baseball memorabilia, easy to understand and appreciate for both pickers and fans interested in starting or expanding their own collections.

Before we get fully underway, two things: First, how do we define that term, "collector?" I think a good working definition is someone who has five or more items of a specific type, whether they're signed baseballs, game-used jerseys, or Willie Mays baseball cards. If you need all your fingers to count up the number of tickets you've saved from the ballpark, or the bobbing head dolls that sit on your mantle, then you're already a collector. Heck, you're a veteran. And if you don't need all five fingers? Then you have the great pleasure of a beautiful beginning.

Second, let's define the difference between the terms "collectible" and "memorabilia." I use them interchangeably throughout this book because you really have to split hairs to define them separately. With that in mind, a "collectible" is any sports-related item that an individual may want, while "memorabilia" is an item associated with a particular team, player, stadium, arena, or event.

Promotional items provided free to fans of all sports—or sold to them—have become highly prized artifacts of American culture.

The Hartland Plastic Company of Hartland, Wis., sold a set of baseball figurines from both leagues with names that are familiar to even casual followers of what was then deemed America's favorite pastime. The American Leaguers were Ted Williams, Al Kaline, Nelson Fox, Yogi Berra, Mickey Mantle, Rocky Colovito, Roger Maris, Harmon Killebrew, and Babe Ruth. The National Leaguers were Henry Aaron, Willie Mays, Duke Snider, Ernie Banks, Warren Spahn, Don Drysdale, Dick Groat, Stan Musial, and Eddie Mathews.

If I were to ask you which one of those figurines is now the most valuable, I'm guessing you'd say Babe Ruth or Mickey Mantle, which would be true with many other collectibles of

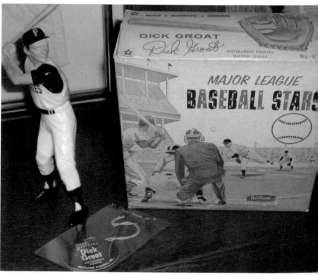

Dick Groat Hartland statue, with original box and tag. The Hartland baseball series of statues were sold in stores from 1958 through 1962 at $1.99 each.

Jeff Figler

those two stars, such as the baseball cards that feature them. But, in this case, the most highly prized figurine is the one depicting Dick Groat, who, though a successful player—an MVP for the Pittsburgh Pirates in 1960—was hardly a household name. Why does his value top the names of such superstars? Simple: Only 5,000 of Groat's figurines were ever made, compared to 50,000, or more, of the others. A pristine Groat statue is worth about $3,000. Get his signature on it—he's a broadcaster for the University of Pittsburgh basketball team—and it's worth even more. Have the statue in the original box with the price tag and it could easily be worth $6,000. Please keep in mind that the Hartland statues of Groat were originally priced modestly, like most toys of that era.

No matter the memorabilia in question, the value of an item is the amount of money someone is willing to pay for it. That may seem obvious, but it's easy to forget that truism when a price guide says the MLB jersey you've owned for two or three decades is worth $1,000, and no one wants to pay you even half that amount when you put it up for sale. So remember that maxim, along with this one: while there are some good price guides out there, the prices listed in them will generally be greater than what you will actually get for your treasures on the open market. Of course, the reverse is true, too: you'll be able to buy many items for less than a glance at the guide might suggest.

FACTORS THAT DETERMINE PRICE

There are three major factors that determine price: condition, scarcity, and desirability.

CONDITION

Condition is as critical to collecting as location is to real estate. Baseball card purists break "condition" into poor, fair, good, very good, excellent, near mint, and mint. There are also shades of each condition, such as VG-EX, for Very Good-Excellent. If a card is graded, for example, by Sportscard Guaranty Corporation (SGC) or Professional Sports Authenticators (PSA), it may make a world of difference as to how the card is valued.

But for our purposes, remember that condition plays a vital role in determining price. An exception often occurs if an item is so rare that its condition won't necessarily matter that much.

Circa 1955 Jackie Robinson single-signed baseball, his blue ink inscription and autograph surviving at 9/10 boldness on the same ONL (Giles) format used throughout the second half of Robinson's decorated career, **$33,460**.

Heritage Auctions

SCARCITY

Ah, yes, *finding* the prize. That brings up scarcity as a determinant of value. For example, a Honus Wagner T206 baseball card will be worth lots of money—even millions—because there are so few of them. It's a Holy Grail among sports collectibles. Another Holy Grail is a Jackie Robinson-signed baseball. Collectors know that a Robinson item is valuable, in large part, because they are scarce. A signed Robinson ball is worth well over several thousand dollars even if it is inscribed to an individual, which generally drives down the value of a signed ball.

Likewise, if an item is plentiful, then the value goes down. Let's take baseball Hall of Famers Stan Musial and Tony Gwynn. They are often compared with each other because they both batted left-handed, remained with one team throughout their careers, and each had more than 3,000 hits. Musial won seven National League batting titles, Gwynn eight. However, because they were so generous with their autographs, their signed items are easy to obtain. A Musial or Gwynn signed baseball may sell for only $45. Clearly, if there were fewer of them, the price would increase to upwards of $100 or more.

People often ask whether having a star add "HOF" (Hall of Fame) and his induction year to his signature adds value to the item. The answer is a qualified yes. The value of, let's say, a ball, will increase by about one and a half times during the first year after their induction. (Yes, collectors really have calibrated it that closely). So, for example, when Gwynn was inducted into the Baseball Hall of Fame in 2007, for the next year the value of his signed ball with the added "HOF 2007" increased. However, after that time, it settled back to where it was before. Why? It's the novelty of having a ball with the letters HOF and the year of induction. But what happens to all forms of novelty? That's right, they wear off. Collectors, like fashionistas, like to be the first, or one of the first, to have something new and unique. As with adding a Hall of Fame year, Gwynn's memorabilia will increase temporarily due to his recent death.

Official NL William White baseball signed by Tony Gwynn on the sweet spot in blue pen, **$30**.

Fusco Auctions

DESIRABILITY

Desirability is the third major component that affects the value of an item. While condition and scarcity are usually measurable, desirability is subjective and personal. For example, a baseball signed by David Ortiz of the Boston Red Sox or a bat signed by the Minnesota Twins' Joe Mauer is likely to be more valuable to some people than to others. That is to be expected with any item. Therefore, it follows that a collector who covets that signed baseball will pay more for it than someone whose passion isn't so easily fired by memorabilia. Then there IS widely renowned memorabilia that almost every sports collector desires. One of them, no matter the condition, is that T206 Honus Wagner baseball card. However, not too many collectors are willing to spend the hundreds of thousands of dollars it takes to own even a low-grade Wagner card. But, when a T206 Wagner does become available, the value is driven sky high because there are enough hard-core collectors vying for it. That card makes me realize that the old saying, "The difference between men and boys is the cost of their toys," is all-too-true. I add a caveat, though: nowadays, there are lots of women collecting sports memorabilia. In fact, when I give presentations on sports collecting, at least a third of the audience is female.

It's impossible to pinpoint the number of people collecting sports memorabilia, but "millions" would be a conservative guess for collectors of all types, and based on my considerable experience, a sizeable percentage of them focus on sports items.

Why? I boil down the answer to four main motivations: 1) particular sports items can provide a tangible connection to one's childhood; 2) an admiration for the durability or uniqueness of old sports items; 3) the investment potential of collecting sports memorabilia; and 4) the simple, unabashed fun of collecting, the *journey* as so many collectors call it.

I listed the connection to childhood first because after interviewing scores of collectors over the years, that's the dominant theme that comes up time and again. I have a deep connection to St. Louis, which drives my own interests in collecting. I follow the St. Louis Cardinals baseball team and the football St. Louis Cardinals, now the Arizona Cardinals. Whenever I see items from those teams, especially from the teams of the 1960s, when I was coming of age, I almost always think about acquiring them.

Most sports collectors have similar feelings about the teams they rooted for in their youth, but the most fanatical fans—the ones who might as well have their team identities branded on their skin—seem to hail from the Big Apple. I'm not sure what it is, but fans of the New York teams give real meaning to loyalty. Maybe it has something to do with growing up with the greatest athletes of so many eras right at their figurative doorstep, men like Joe DiMaggio, Jackie Robinson, Mickey Mantle, and Roger Maris. Those are some of the names who have turbo-charged baseball collecting over the decades.

The second reason I cited—admiration for products of the

Four Players Who Have Turbo-Charged Collecting

A 1939 Play Ball Joe DiMaggio #26 HOF rookie card, EX+, **$650**.

William Bunch Auctions & Appraisals

A 1961 Topps Roger Maris #2 signed card, EX condition and signed in bold blue Sharpie, **$657.25**.

Heritage Auctions

Mickey Mantle signed replica *Sports Illustrated* cover, features a photograph of a young Mantle in the heat of his race to baseball's triple crown, originally released by Upper Deck, authenticated, and signed by Mantle in blue Sharpie (10). Sold as part of a lot that also included a signed postcard from Mickey Mantle's restaurant and a grouping of three precious metal baseball cards by Sport Strikes and Enviromint, **$650**.

Geppi's Memorabilia Road Show

A 1952 Topps #312 Jackie Robinson in a PSA graded holder, VG/EX4, **$750**.

Conestoga Auction Company

past—becomes more apparent to collectors as they gain experience. Many collectors, including me, think the gray flannel jersey worn by players in earlier decades was a better product than the fabric used today. Along the same lines, the sports cards of earlier eras, particularly the Topps sets from the early to mid-1950s, seemed to have more visual appeal than their recent counterparts. That certainly spurred Topps, in 2008, to issue cards of current players that maintained the same visual attractiveness of the 1952, 1955, and 1956 sets.

Now let's look at the investment angles. First, let me say that I do not advocate collecting for this reason. I can't be any clearer than that. That said, I don't have a problem with people who include sports memorabilia in their investment portfolio, and more than one pro collector has told me that his collectibles outperform his other investments on a consistent basis. That's because collecting with an eye on favorable returns works only for high-end items—those that cost, at the very least, thousands of dollars and, in some cases, *millions*. But if your pockets are deep enough to afford a Wagner baseball card, a Jackie Robinson signed baseball, or a Lou Gehrig game-used jersey, you're likely to see at least 10 to 15 percent appreciation each year, even in a poor economy.

Prices can be misleading, though, because bidding wars often dictate the final sale price. But it is fair to say that high-end items can easily outperform stocks, bonds, and real estate, even in bullish times.

But sometimes shocking developments can bring down prices almost overnight. Take, for example, the memorabilia of baseball players Barry Bonds, Mark McGwire, Roger Clemens, Sammy Sosa, and even Rafael Palmeiro. All of those men have suffered a serious fall from grace—and so has the value of their memorabilia, which, to put it kindly, nosedived when the bad news surfaced. Am I exaggerating? Not in the least. Sports memorabilia dealers command only about 25 percent of the prices for items from those tarnished stars of the diamond. Investors who banked on the stock of those players rising forever were hit with a painful jolt of reality. Big spender Todd McFarlane paid $3.1 million in 1998 for McGwire's 70th home run ball of 1998. That ball might be worth a third of that amount now.

In short, collecting sports memorabilia is hardly risk free.

The final reason I offer for collecting is to have fun. More than any other suggestion I'll make in the pages that follow, I urge you to collect what you enjoy owning. If you enjoyed the New York Mets, then collect cards of that team. After all, who will ever forget "Marvelous" Marv Thornberry? Well, probably a lot of people, but if he's one of your favorites, then by all means collect his memorabilia.

As you begin to collect, I can almost promise you that you'll notice other collectors all around you. Friends, family members, associates at work, will all begin to reveal themselves as collectors. How do I know? It happened to me and to most of the collectors whom I've met over the years.

It started with my own mother. I began to notice that she had the most amazing collection of refrigerator magnets from far-flung places to cover the entire front of her fridge. She also saved huge collections of my baseball cards and comic books from my childhood, which jump-started my collecting obsession as an adult. Then, when my son was old enough to enjoy sporting events, the two of us started collecting not only sports cards together, but also *Star Wars* cards, which he loved. My son and I are still collecting memorabilia together many years later. To share a passion with my child is one of the greatest gifts life has given me. My wife is an avid collector as well—of masks, and, would you believe, witches? She has more than two hundred big and small witches. She does not believe in voodoo, thank goodness, or I might worry about the Jeff Figler doll she has on a shelf that's right next to a gnarly-looking set of pins. As my wife once told me as she gazed at a roomful of my collectibles, "If you can't beat them, join them."

I've been down this road for many years, and I've learned a great deal about collecting, mostly through trial and error. I never had the benefit of a guide or mentor to bring me along. That's what I'd like to be for you, so you can learn from my mistakes.

Thanks for taking me along on your ride.

The great Babe Ruth is one of the most, if not *the* most, collectible baseball player. This 1916 photo of Ruth as a member of the Boston Red Sox sold at auction for **$17,925**.

Heritage Auctions

CHAPTER 1

The Who, What, and How of Baseball Picking and Collecting

Ask a hundred experts for their list of the most collectible baseball athletes and I'm guessing no two lists will look the same. Sure, there will be some consensus, but a lot of diverging opinions as well.

SOME OF THE MOST COLLECTIBLE PLAYERS

With that in mind, the fact that President Franklin Roosevelt insisted that baseball continue during World War II gives you some measure of how close to the pulse of the United States the great game has always been. And if we have to point to one player for whom the consensus is strongest, it would have to be the incomparable George Herman "Babe" Ruth.

Ruth joined the game just when baseball needed a lift, and he certainly proved to be the right player at the right time. Legends soon arose around the Babe, and he did little to discourage them, which from a collector's point of view was just fine, because as it raised his stock, it raised the value of everything associated with the man. A *lot* was associated with Ruth in the way of collectibles because he was a most prolific autograph signer. That means there is still a great deal of Ruth memorabilia that can be had for the right price.

Ruth-signed baseballs run the spectrum. Major auction houses have sold them for anywhere from $5,000 to more than $70,000, even more. What else is out there? How about a Ruth-signed 1938 World Series program that went for nearly $3,000, or a *Look* magazine that fetched even more. Baseball cards of Ruth can cost well over $30,000; that was the case with a 1916 rookie card.

Ruth often signed baseballs with other players; perhaps most notably, Lou Gehrig. A ball signed by both of those superstars is generally worth more than a ball signed just by Ruth. Team baseballs, such as the ones of the 1927 New York Yankees—with both Ruth and Gehrig—or the 1915 Boston Red Sox, are both extremely valuable. Of course, the "called shot" homer by Ruth in the 1932 World Series off of Cubs' pitcher Charlie Root would garner the most money of any Ruth ball— by far—but until it emerges, that's an unsolved mystery.

While Babe Ruth is, without a doubt, the most collectible baseball player, the consensus surely places Mickey Mantle in the baseball pantheon. "The Mick" ended his illustrious career in 1969. His fame was far-reaching, but he was injury prone, and that cut short his career. He arrived in the big leagues and had to perform on the world's largest stage—Yankee Stadium— *and* replace a national icon—Joe DiMaggio, aka the husband, for a while, of Marilyn Monroe. Mantle was nicknamed the "Commerce Comet" because he came of age in Commerce, Oklahoma. He certainly burst on the national scene, and his popularity, to judge only from the value of his collectibles, has never waned.

In fact, Mantle's rookie card, the 1952 Topps card number 311, is considered the second most valuable baseball card of all time, topped only by the "Holy Grail" of sports cards, the T206 Honus Wagner (see the Mantle card on Page 50 and the Wagner card on Pages 57-59). One of Mantle's Topps 311 cards was auctioned for about $250,000. Others go for considerably less, but can still reach the $50,000 to $80,000 range. There's an intriguing story about that 1952 Topps baseball card. Card sales were sluggish toward the end of the 1952 summer, so Topps decided to empty the remaining inventory of them into the Atlantic Ocean, instead of keeping them in storage. Of course, included in the dumped cards were scores of Mantle's rookie card. That meant far fewer were ever in circulation, which further limits their number today. The old economic theory of supply and demand was vindicated, once again, in the high prices accorded Mantle's premier card.

Most other Mantle memorabilia costs far less. Take, for example, an original Hartland statue. A Mantle Hartland will cost around $1,500. Ruth's Hartland in the same condition? $300. Go figure. Perhaps the disparity, at least as far as the Hartland statue is concerned, can be explained by Mantle's great popularity among baby boomers, millions of whom grew up watching him roam the outfield grass of Yankee Stadium, and in later years, the first base territory. In his prime, he could run like a gazelle, and many experts consider him the greatest switch hitter of all time. He sure sparked an interest in batting from both sides of the plate among his many fans.

How about a short list of the most collectible current baseball players? I'd include Derek Jeter, and a tad further down, Yasiel Puig and Albert Pujols, Clayton Kershaw and Miguel Cabrera. Of that group, Jeter and Puig dominate today's market. And to pick from only those two, I'd go with Jeter as the single most collectible contemporary player.

Jeter's stats from his magnificent career are arguably some of the greatest in baseball history, experts predict that he could become the top right-handed batter of all time, with Ted Williams still holding that distinction among left- handed hitters.

So jump on the opportunity to pick any Jeter or Puig item, especially ones that are signed, and then make sure you include them in your will. Signed, game-used Jeter or Pujols jerseys may easily double in value, especially if Pujols' statistics continue to impress, not least of which is his relentless home-run march that could lift him past the all-time record held by Barry Bonds. Signed, game-used bats of his have sold for nearly $5,000, and signed balls for several hundred dollars. Much of his new memorabilia is controlled by his foundation, but items can still be acquired through auctions and other venues.

Having retired, Jeter, of course, is now a Yankee icon, which automatically lifts him onto an exclusive list. The fact that he has passed the 3,000 hits mark, and that he is a surefire first ballot Hall of Famer, increases his popularity well beyond the borders of the Big Apple.

Pujols, Kershaw and Cabrera are highly collectible, and their memorabilia should be considered, even by beginning collectors and pickers. Rivera will join Jeter in the Hall of Fame.

As a collector of baseballs, I'd love to be able to predict who will become stars from the first day they debut, but it's not

Derek Jeter is one of the top modern baseball players who is highly collectible. This photo of his grand-slam moment in 2005 was included with his game-worn jersey put up for auction earlier this year. To find out what it sold for, see Page 106.

Heritage Auctions

that easy, is it? Sports collectors thought they had a sure-shot with Stephen Strasburg. The former collegiate standout at San Diego State University signed with the Washington Nationals, and broke collecting records galore with his debut. Then he got injured, so the jury is now out on Strasburg collectibles. His Nationals teammate, Bryce Harper, may turn out to be highly collectible himself.

WHAT TO COLLECT

There are dozens of baseball collectibles, with one universal: the baseball. Not only do baseball players sign them, but athletes from all other sports sign them as well. Celebrities of every stripe and generation sign baseballs, too, from Frank Sinatra to Bob Dylan. The baseball, as a medium for autographs, transcends the diamond. I have seen baseballs signed by presidents, entertainers, actors, business people, religious leaders, and even dictators.

There is quite a bit of overlap among sports collectibles. Also, most of the items noted may be signed or unsigned. Please keep in mind as you go through the list that it is not all-inclusive. But, with a few exceptions, these are the collectibles noted in the book because they will be the overwhelming majority of the collectibles that you will come across in your sports collecting and picking journey: cards, jerseys and uniforms, baseballs, gloves, bats, photos, artwork, board games and other games, batting helmets, bobbing head dolls, figurines, pins, pennants, programs, jewelry, stadium seats, tickets, media

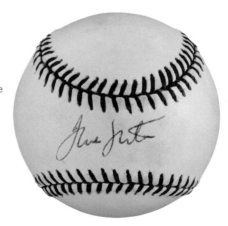

Circa 1995 Frank Sinatra single-signed baseball. The king of crooners, "Ol' Blue Eyes" himself, was known as one of the most popular singers in American history, **$2,868**.

Heritage Auctions

guides and magazines, and movie posters from baseball films such as *Field of Dreams, Bull Durham, For the Love of the Game,* and *The Upside of Anger* (and those are just Kevin Costner's baseball flicks).

Even when I'm hosting a radio show about sports collectibles, or on as a guest, I hear from listeners who want to tell me about their collections of rulers, ashtrays, posters, mugs, glasses, board games, playing cards, you name it. But keeping the callers to the subject at hand, when it's about sports, has its rewards; sometimes very rich ones.

A woman called KMOX radio in St. Louis not too long ago claiming that she was given one of Willie Mays' gloves. Not just any glove, either. She said it was the one the "Say Hey Kid" of the New York Giants used to catch the ball slammed by Vic Wertz of the Cleveland Indians in the first game of the 1954 World Series. My ears sure perked up. That glove played the central role in the most famous over-the-shoulder catch that Mays ever made. Some renowned sports enthusiasts call it the greatest grab of all time.

The woman said that a relative gave her the glove, and she wanted to know its value. To be honest, I was as dubious that she owned the glove, so I asked her more about it. The more she talked, the more convinced I became that she had the real deal. Moreover, she wasn't trying to drum up interest for a sale because she wanted to hang onto it, kind of like Mays hung onto the ball that once smacked deep into its pocket. Good for her, I thought. She just wanted to know its value.

I had to think about that one before I gave her my answer: $350,000. That would make it one of the highest priced collectibles in all of sports, but that glove is a unique gem, another one of the Holy Grails of sports.

In contrast to that inquisitive woman, most callers hope that their memorabilia is worth more than it really is, and I usually become the bearer of bad news, though as often as not. I reserve judgment because it's difficult to appraise an item if you haven't seen it. That's especially true when you remember how critical condition is to the worth of almost any item. Notice I said "almost"; the Mays glove is such a treasure that condition would hardly rank as much of a factor.

I encourage people to email me photos of their most cherished collectibles, if they want to know what they're worth.

This is not the 1954 game-used glove of Willie Mays, but a 1964 game-used one that also sold for a pretty penny. A vintage number "24" appears in marker on the exterior thumb, with "24 Willie Mays" applied in the same marker to the pinky and ring finger, **$15,535**.

Heritage Auctions

It's not a perfect system, but it works better than describing it verbally. You're welcome to do the same: collectingwithjeff@ sbcglobal.net.

Before I give my presentation to groups of sports collectors, I encourage them to bring a couple of the items they hold most dear, if they want my opinion of their value. I have seen some spectacular collectibles. I had one woman who showed up with a stack of World Series programs from every single game in which the St. Louis Cardinals played—and there have been many of them. Those programs dated back to the 1920s, and they were in pristine condition.

More often, I have to tell people that the promotional items given away at a stadium generally aren't worth much, even if you have several of them. And that includes bobbing head dolls—unless you plan to keep them fifty years with the hope that you'll have one of a kind. Patience may be a virtue, but in a case like that, patience would be truly overrated. But, hey, bobbing head dolls are wonderful souvenirs and should be relished for what they are—a memory of a great day at the ballpark.

Whether you're a Chicago Cubs season ticket holder, or a

Steps to Take to Begin Your Journey as a Baseball Collector

- Think about what interests you and make a list.
- Decide on the size of your budget.
- Determine if what you want to collect is even possible.
- Ask yourself how you will obtain your desired items.
- Ask yourself if you have the space necessary to display your items.
- Ask yourself if you're willing to keep good records of what you collect, including pictures and provenance.

Los Angeles Dodgers supporter, the steps you take to become a collector of baseball memorabilia remain essentially the same. You should first focus on your interests and making a list. That may sound simple, but don't underestimate the importance of your first step because it will be vital to your success, and not making any costly mistakes.

A little guidance is in order. Most collectors acquire memorabilia related to a specific player, team, item, or the city from which the team hails. Think about your own allegiances. What stirs your memories most? Were the Boston Red Sox your favorite team when you were growing up? The Kansas City Royals? The San Francisco Giants?

Maybe you plan on keeping your collection small, perhaps just a set of autographed glossy photos of players or game programs. You might even consider jerseys, if they fit into your budget plans.

Los Angeles is just one of the many great sports towns in the U.S. Baltimore also ranks right up with the best. If the Orioles get your blood pumping, consider focusing on those teams and the memorabilia of Cal Ripken, Jr.

You can focus your acquisitions in any number of ways. You

might choose to have your collection zero in on a single year in a team's history. The 1968 Detroit Tigers marched to the World Series on the strength of Denny McClain's pitching. He won 31 games that year, a record unlikely to be eclipsed anytime soon, though it was teammate, Mickey Lolich, who was the World Series star in the team's upset of the Bob Gibson-led St. Louis Cardinals. That famed Redbirds team was trying to repeat as world champs. They failed, but few sports fans can forget that the team with Gibson, Curt Flood, and Lou Brock did make it to three World Series during the five-year period from 1964 to 1968.

Lot of one *1968 Detroit Tigers World Series Program* and World Series Ticket game 3; also one St. Louis Cardinals' Busch Stadium 1968 World Series ticket stub, game 2, **$175**.

DuMouchelles

In general, I recommend that collectors focus on one or two types of items, but challenges arise even with a narrow focus. For instance, anyone who wants to collect every single baseball card ever issued faces a major hurdle, especially if their goal includes going after all the pre-1900 cards. That's not even taking into account the bewildering array of cards issued since then, which would include all the Topps, Fleer, Bowman, etc. cards, along with all the sets that companies such as Upper Deck and Panini still issue. Just about impossible.

What I've done—and many other collectors have as well—is to acquire all of a particular manufacturer's cards in a specific sport. Let's say you want to collect all the Topps baseball cards from their first issues in 1952. That's a practical goal. Once you've gathered up all the old sets, all you have to do is order a factory set every year to keep your collection current.

Some collectors, would-be collectors, and pikers subscribe to sports magazines or newsletters, including online varieties of both, to give them an idea of what they might want to collect or pick. I don't dismiss this approach at all, but I would caution anyone adopting this tactic to still make sure that they're strongly drawn to whatever they decide to acquire. Make sure the items catch more than your eye—that they catch your heart. If you don't, your interest might well flag.

I've seen this happen many times, and not just in sports collecting. Ask anyone collecting memorabilia—stamps, coins, movie posters, props, records, or anything else—and they will tell you that to collect successfully, you must have the passion that I mention so often. I still get a real thrill every time I see a piece of my collection in the Figler Museum or in my office.

A significant part of that thrill comes from knowing how I acquired every single item. Now, some collectors and pikers buy other people's complete collections, which in my opinion is fair game. Frankly, it's a smart approach if the collection you're eyeing so closely is just what you want. It's not my approach, but I understand the appeal and see the wisdom in some circumstances, as I do with pickers who adopt the hobby purely for investment purposes. While investing might appear bloodless to so many aficionados, the reality, as noted earlier, is that high-end items can appreciate considerably every year, notwithstanding the plummeting value of the memorabilia of those embroiled in professional or personal scandals (McGwire, Clemens, Sosa, Bonds, and others). But, let's face it, if your walls sport a McGwire game-used jersey, or even a LeRoy Neiman portrait of the fallen star, you've got a great conversation piece, though I suspect the professional investor would find a chatty moment or two a shallow substitute for financial gain. (Little did McGwire realize when he refused to discuss steroid use before a Congressional committee that investors in his memorabilia would be so financially impacted. Ditto for Clemens and his collectibles.)

For the professional investor and pickers, a much safer approach is to acquire vintage items. While the reputations of the dead occasionally become tarred, that's rare, and rarer still is a drop in the value of their items. This is especially true when

If Luis Gonzalez's used bubble gum isn't to your liking, how about a signed jersey instead? A 2005 American and National League All-Star signed jersey, **$175**.

Geppi's Memorabilia Road Show

Pricey Bubble Gum

Whichever team you focus on, you can buy jerseys, balls, programs, whatever is associated with the players and their game. In fact—and this is positively bewildering—you can even collect the remains of a player's gum. That's right. Two pieces of bubble gum chewed by former Arizona Diamondbacks outfielder Luis Gonzalez sold for $10,000. Who'd have thunk that garbage could be worth so much? But it is, though I don't know yet of another collector who has actually acquired more than one piece of chewed-up gum, and I'm not sure I'd race off to see the display, even if it did become available.

LeRoy Neiman "Mark McGwire" painting, hand signed by the artist, limited edition offset lithograph limited to 5,000, 24" x 36", sold at a 2013 auction for **$200**.

Windsor Auction

you're talking about revered memorabilia, such as the Honus Wagner T206 card. Keep a card like that, even for a year or two, and you will be pleasantly rewarded, regardless of the card's condition at the time of purchase. That's assuming, of course, that you did not grossly overpay for such an item in the first place.

Time for full disclosure: I bought a Honus Wagner T206 card a number of years ago. Notice, please, that I said I "bought," not that I "invested" in a Wagner. For me, finally acquiring a Wagner was the pinnacle of my career as a collector. It is, without doubt, the Holy Grail of sports cards; and I knew it would provide the cornerstone of my museum, the lure that would bring in visitors and money for the children's charities that I support. Because of that, I must admit that I sometimes worry that a new cache of Wagners will be found in someone's basement or attic, which would immediately pull the carpet out from the value of the presently known cards. But I don't lose sleep over that possibility; neither do I sit around trying to calculate the increasing value of my card as the years fly by. Most days, though, I do let my eyes settle on it for a few moments, for it represents to me the inestimable honor of baseball, its rich history and vibrant future. Call me a sentimentalist, but that's how I feel. I suspect I'm not alone. That's why I rarely part with any item I've collected, even when the overtures from potential buyers are strong. Case in point: my baseball signed by all the big stars of *The Wizard of Oz*. Remember my saying that baseballs are famous for being signed by celebrities of all types? That ball of mine is a sterling example. It has the autographs of Bert Lahr, Jack Haley, Frank Morgan, and, of course, the lady herself, Judy Garland. An old friend of mine, baseball agent Andy Strasburg, once asked me what it would take for me to part with the ball. I was pretty sure Andy was inquiring on behalf of his client, baseball superstar and Hall of Famer Ozzie Smith, whose nickname is "The Wizard of Oz." Much as I would have liked to oblige Andy, I couldn't give up the ball, and it remains in the Figler Museum.

I've also heard from professional investors over the years, and I've turned them down, too. Undoubtedly, some of them found the treasures they were looking for elsewhere; I know for certain that Wagners, for instance, have been scooped up by professionals. Those higher-end items always will be. But not all of the latter are in the million-dollar range. Not even close. Game-used jerseys once worn by Sandy Koufax, Lou Gehrig, Ted Williams, and many other superstars are all reasonable—and solid—investments.

Sandy Koufax game-used jersey, 1965, **$262,900**.

Jeff Figler

SETTING A BUDGET

Woe unto those who do not heed the following admonition:
determining your collectibles budget is critical, not only to the
scope and magnitude of your collection, but to your ultimate
happiness. Am I overstating the case? Going over-the-top? Not
in the least. Let's start with the impact collecting could have on
your spouse or lifetime companion. I have known more than
a few collectors who have actually spent so much money on
their obsessions that their spouses and significant others have
walked out on them, leaving them with considerable holdings
of a material sort, but a darn sight poorer emotionally.

You have to control your collecting. At the risk of stating the
obvious, don't let it control you. It's easy to get so carried away
that you neglect the most important aspects of your life.

It helps to have a spouse or partner who is supportive of
your hobby, as my wife is of mine. She recognizes the value
of having the museum, and I do my best to reciprocate with
interest in her collections. But what truly complicates a budget
isn't your significant other—it's your own emotions. Here's a
common scenario for how quickly and *dangerously* you can

lose control of your emotions in the collecting game.

Let's say that for years you've been a big fan of first base-man Prince Fielder of the Texas Rangers, and now that you're a collector, you find that one of his game-used jerseys for the Rangers or his previous teams, Milwaukee Brewers or Detroit Tigers, is up for auction. Right away, you know this could be costly. You've sat down with your spouse and the two of you have agreed to a $500 monthly budget for acquiring items. This is a lot of money for the two of you, and it means sacrificing other pleasures on which you've spent your disposable income, including going out for a weekly romantic dinner. But she's got your back—as long as you stick to the budget.

The minimum bid for the Fielder jersey is $300. That's in your ballpark. Maybe you'll get lucky and the bids won't go too high. Maybe you'll even be able to snag Fielder's jersey for a single month of your budget. Maybe, maybe, maybe. But you "need" that Fielder jersey! You've talked up your collecting to your friends, and wouldn't it be grand to have them come over and see the Fielder jersey hanging on your wall? Why, you even met Prince's estranged father, Cecil, years ago when he was with the Tigers—and still on speaking terms with his son.

The online bidding starts slowly. You hold off, encouraged when it goes only to $450. That's when you join the action by bidding $500. There, you've done it. Now, you wait. Oops! Not for long. Other bidders come crashing in from virtual space, and now the high bid has leaped to $2,200. It's a frenzy. You feel your heart pumping. Your palms are damp. No, they're wring-ing wet. You've never experienced anything like this, not even at the blackjack table. Prince Fielder is a bona fide star, a mega-millionaire who's earned every dollar he's paid. You *want* that jersey. But your hopes of acquiring it with your $500 a month have been dashed in a hurry—in minutes!

Should you even risk bidding again? No, of course not. But when will one of his jerseys ever come up for auction again? Maybe never. It's not like you can cruise down to Walmart and say, "Hey, I'll take that game-used Prince Fielder jersey with the garden hoe."

Already, you're re-budgeting. You're thinking, well, $500 a month times five months is more than the $2,200 that the jersey might go for. In for a penny, in for a pound, right?

So you bid, and then you bid again. Things get a little blurry at this point, and by the time your feet are planted firmly back on the ground, you're the high bidder at $4,000. Congratulations you've won the Prince Fielder game-used jersey. You beat out everyone else.

Right about then, your sweet supportive wife comes in and says, "How did it go, honey?"

You thought your hands were wet earlier, your palms greasy, your heart on the fast track to cardiac arrest? That's nothing, buddy. Wait till you have to tell her that you paid *$4,000* for a sweaty jersey because that's how she's going to look at it, and you know that's exactly what she'll be thinking by the suddenly hard glint in her eye. Yes, it's there before you can say a word, and then she does say a word—five of them: "How *much* did you pay?"

There goes the kids' trip to Disneyland, or the vacation you promised her in Kauai. Go ahead, fess up, *maybe* she'll understand.

You get the picture? You see how fast it can all go south?

If you absolutely do not need a Prince Fielder game-used jersey and can settle for a signed one instead, you can save yourself a lot of money – and potential trouble with your spouse. This "Majestic [size] 48" jersey, signed on the back number in mint silver Sharpie when Fielder played for the Milwaukee Brewers, sold at auction for **$125.48**.

Heritage Auctions

Don't let it happen, friend. No collectible is worth it. That's why *sticking* to your budget is critical. Determining it is not an exercise in futility; it's a critical part of who you are and what you'll become. The same principle applies regardless of your budget, whether it's $100 a month or $1,000.

Look, if you have the money, and it won't upset other plans, go for it. If not, hold off. I know just how tough that call can be. One time I held off buying a 1953 St. Louis Browns signed baseball. That was a significant year because it was the last season the team played in St. Louis before moving to Baltimore, later to be renamed the Orioles. I consoled myself by thinking that I'd see another 1953 Browns ball come up for sale in the next few months, at the latest.

Things did not work out quite that smoothly. For three years I looked in every auction catalog I could find and conducted online searches. Not ... a ... thing. When I finally came across another 1953 Browns ball, I scooped it right up and paid plenty for it, more than I might have in that original auction. So that's the other side of the coin: sometimes if you don't bid, you end up paying more than you ever bargained for.

But these tough calls help make collecting so exciting. Just be realistic about your budget, and if you can't control yourself, find a less injurious way to occupy yourself. That couch can get cold.

The other factor to keep in mind is that you can always adjust your budget, and I don't mean during those frenzied moments when you're bidding. I mean in a cool, calculated manner. It's best to start off with a conservative figure, increasing it as you can. Remember, the easiest thing is adjusting to a higher standard of living.

Your budget should include more than just the money you'll need to acquire items. Sometimes there are travel expenses, if you're going to personally attend auctions, which is fun. And there are costs to displaying your collection handsomely.

There's one other budget to keep in mind: your time. You don't want to ignore your family because you're working on your collection. Don't hide out in your "man cave," or "woman cave," as the case may be. Come up for air, take a deep breath, enjoy your real treasures: your loved ones.

IS IT EVEN COLLECTIBLE?

There are items so rare that they never come up for auction.

They sit in revered places like the Baseball Hall of Fame in Cooperstown, New York. Other memorabilia comes up for auction every decade or so, and costs so much that most of us just shake our heads in wonder. I've noted a few of those, so I won't belabor that point.

More modestly priced items are, naturally, easier to find. For example, if you're looking to acquire all the baseball cards of the 2005 Toronto Blue Jays, a phone call or two will probably net you want you want. Most sports cards are not vintage and extremely valuable like the T206 Honus Wagner, 1952 Topps 311 Mickey Mantle, and some of the Babe Ruth cards in top condition are, so as long as you're not trying to play in that league, you'll be able to obtain cards for a reasonable price.

You can easily pick up a resource guide of people in the industry who will gladly help you. These folks often are affiliated with auction houses, websites, local retailers, or collectors who are active buying and selling sports memorabilia. Lou Criscione of Inside the Park Collectibles is an expert on bobbing head dolls and figurines. Bill Goodwin of Goodwin and Company can tell you about vintage baseball cards. My experience with these guys, and many others in the industry, is that they are extremely candid, and will even assist you in finding items on your "wish list," if they don't have the memorabilia themselves.

Collectors of all types draw up a "wish list" of items that they want, then distribute the "list" to people whom they think can find them. In time, most things are possible—unless Cooperstown beats you to the punch.

AMAZING TREASURES STILL WAITING TO BE DISCOVERED

Do you know who Bernice Gallegos is? Don't feel bad, most people don't. But after you read what I'm about to tell you, you'll wish you had her luck and pluck.

Bernice is an antiques dealer. With her husband, Al, she owns Collectique in the Tower District of Fresno, California.

In 2008, Bernice reached into a box and pulled out a baseball card. Not so unusual; if you deal in antiques or other used items, you come across all kinds of oddities, but rarely one quite like the treasure Bernice found. The card said, "Red Stock B.B. Club of Cincinnati," and showed ten men in baseball uniforms, with their socks pulled up to their knees. She knew the card was old, and figured it was a prime candidate for eBay.

Now, here's where the story gets even more interesting. She was going to start the card on eBay at $15, but to save *twenty* cents, she put it up with a description and a $10 price tag. Lo and behold, that same night she received a few inquiries asking her about the card's authenticity. When one potential buyer asked her to end the auction immediately and sell him the card, Bernice had a feeling that it might be worth more than she thought, maybe even $25. Fancy that.

But when the inquires kept coming, she pulled the card from the auction and decided some due diligence was in order. Here's what she found: The card was from 1869, and was an advertisement for Peck & Snyder, a New York sports equipment company. And, as you might already know, the team featured on it was the Cincinnati Red Stockings, the first professional baseball team.

Bernice was not a baseball fan. She'd never even attended a baseball game of any kind, but she found herself quickly warming up to the national pastime. Money will do that. And Bernice's card was worth a pretty penny because when she had it graded by PSA, the organization confirmed that she had one of the earliest baseball cards ever made.

She put it up for auction with Memory Lane, where it sold for a grand total of $64,073. Add the 17-1/2 percent buyer's premium, and the total climbed to $75,286, the highest price ever paid for the handful of 1869 Peck and Snyder Cincinnati cards that have been auctioned.

Now, many sports history buffs know that before those Cincinnati Red Stockings, there were no professional baseball teams. The Red Stockings formed in 1868 and were led by Hall of Fame brothers George and Harry Wright. The 1869 team featured on the card that Bernice found went undefeated, winning games by as many as fifty runs. Can you imagine that nowadays? The Red Stockings went on to help form what is now Major League Baseball, bringing in players from across the country, who barnstormed from coast to coast.

The Peck & Snyder card was larger than today's cards, but maybe it had to be: it featured the entire team, not individual players.

So just how did Bernice Gallegos and her husband come to own that precious card? They're not exactly sure, but they

This is not Bernice's card, but another Peck & Snyder Cincinnati Red Stockings Team trade card from 1869 that sold in 2011, 3-15/16" x 2-7/16", **$26,290**.

Heritage Auctions

The rare 149-year-old baseball card of the Brooklyn Atlantics amateur baseball club that was found at a yard sale and sold at auction in 2013 for **$92,000**.

Saco River Auction

think it came from the contents of a storage space that they'd bought a few years earlier, which had cost them about $200. They had done that a number of times before, usually making a small profit on their investments. Once they even found a John F. Kennedy autograph from 1939 that they sold on eBay for $1,000. But nothing like that Red Stockings card, which made collectors and pickers green with envy.

It may be hard to believe that an even rarer card was discovered at a yard sale in rural Maine and sold at auction in 2013 for $92,000. The 1865 card depicts the Brooklyn Atlantics amateur baseball club and the winning bidder said he bought it as an investment for his young son.

So what's the takeaway message here? Valuable sports memorabilia is still out there waiting to be found. Maybe it's high time you started cleaning out your basement and attic, and scour those old scrapbooks that have been lying around collecting dust, mildew, and mites for decades. Maybe you should even start buying the contents of abandoned storage units.

One of my fears is that Bernice or someone like her is going to come up with an old cache of T206 Honus Wagner cards. That would drive down the value of my most prized collectible; but let's face it, one of the great things about collecting and picking is the dizzying possibility that great discoveries are just waiting to be found somewhere out there—or in the recesses of your own home.

You might be thinking that Bernice has all the luck. You don't know the half of it. While it might be painful to hear this, I must offer you an astounding footnote to her story: that old baseball card wasn't even her biggest score. Not even close. This is a lady who several years earlier had won $250,000 at a Lake Tahoe casino playing a *quarter* slot machine. Yee gads! Talk about good fortune.

BEST PLACES TO FIND BASEBALL MEMORABILIA

While I've networked with experts in the field, most of the time I adopt a more common approach to finding memorabilia: I take part in telephone or Web auctions, use eBay, attend garage sales and swap meets, scan ads in newspapers and Craigslist, and attend trade shows and conventions.

Let me break this down a little further: For higher-end items, I gravitate toward auctions. For more commonplace memorabilia, I keep a close eye on eBay, though there are some worthy high-end items on eBay as well.

AUCTIONS

A confession: When I first started attending auctions, I was completely naïve. *How* naïve, you might ask? I actually thought that I could retract a bid at any time during an auction. How's that for putting it all out there? Fortunately, people were kind enough not to laugh at me.

That was an easy enough lesson, but a much tougher one is learning when to stop bidding. I cited the example of the individual losing control of himself over a Prince Fielder jersey. Just as common, if not more so, is when you want to kick yourself because it turns out that your last bid was topped only by the winning bid; *if I'd gone just a little bit higher.* Believe me, everybody has had that thought at least once. You can't help but believe that if you had bid one more time the item would have been yours. But it's never that simple because you have no idea how high the other bidder would have gone. You might have ended up like the fellow who found himself the owner of Fielder's jersey—and sleeping on the couch. So don't regret not bidding.

That's a general rule of mine, and it applies to all kinds of auctions—telephone, Internet, and the country-style auctions where you actually show up in person. How do you find out about them? I recommend *Sports Collectors Digest* (sportscollectorsdigest.com), which lists more sports collectibles auctions than any other publication that I know about. It's published biweekly. Auction Report (auctionreport.com) keeps its readers informed about auctions.

So now you've found some auction houses that deal in memorabilia that might interest you. Contact them and ask for their catalogs. The first thing you should do is check the date of the auction to make sure it hasn't already come and gone. Silly as it seems, this does happen, typically if you've been on vacation, or when there's a snafu with the postal system.

Now, if the auction has already been held, you might think you're fat out of luck, but guess what? You could still be in the game because if the auction house states that an item receiving no bids can be purchased for the "reserve amount," (the consignee's lowest acceptable price) it's worth checking to see if the memorabilia that interests you was sold. If not, and you're

Never Pay for a Catalog

Here's a bit of advice that will definitely save you money: never pay for a catalog. NEVER. Catalogs have become works of art and, admittedly, they're expensive to produce. You can't help but be impressed with how beautifully the auction items are presented. Over the years, I've seen these presentations grow ever more lavish. It's as if each auction house feels compelled to outdo all the others. So what's a "poor" auction house to do? Why, pass the cost on to the customers, meaning you, the potential bidder. Don't fall for it.

Sometimes a company will promise that if you're the high bidder on any items, the cost of the catalog will be deducted from your winning bid. Don't fall for it. Or they'll tell you that once you're a high bidder, you'll never have to buy a catalog from them again. Don't fall for it.

The companies say they're trying to weed out the non-serious bidders by charging a fee. But you've got to ask yourself, how can any potential bidder know if he or she's interested in an item if the company doesn't provide them with a catalog? Clearly, they can't.

What should you do if a company flat refuses to give you a catalog? Take your business elsewhere. There are a great many sports auctions to choose from, and you don't have to pay for a catalog. If their short-sighted policies keep you from bidding, that's their loss.

first to contact the house, you might find yourself nabbing a real bargain—*after* the auction has been over for days. There are tricks to this trade, and that's one of them.

A FEE YOU CAN'T AVOID

An auction house fee that you generally can't avoid is the buyer's commission. In the past decade or so, the buyer's commission has become very common. It works like this: Say your winning bid for an item is $100. If the auction house has a buyer's commission of 18 percent, your winning bid will actually cost you $118. Buyer's commissions range from 10 percent to 20 percent, and it goes into the auction house's kitty. Even after paying that fee, there's shipping, insurance, and any applicable state taxes. So you need to think about those additional costs when you're bidding, because they can add up fast.

Auction houses have concluded, rightly so it would appear, that because so many of their catalog items are high-end, bidders will be willing to spend the extra amount necessitated by the buyer's commission. However, I know collectors who have said, in effect, "Enough's enough. I'm not going to pay it." But they are a tiny minority of buyers. To add insult to injury, at least in the view of that tiny minority, most auction houses also charge a seller's commission. That means that if you're the consignor, and the winning bid for your item is $100, a percentage of that figure is deducted from what you'll receive. If the seller's commission was 18 percent, you'd receive $82, not the $100 it actually sold for.

The auction house gets you coming and going. *Ouch-ouch!*

Many auctions have a thirty-minute rule: The rule requires you to place an initial bid before a specified time, if you want to bid during an extended bidding period—when the bidding goes past its scheduled deadline. Think of this rule as the one that says you must be willing to *pay* early in the auction if you want to *play* later.

I've stayed up many hours past my bedtime to nab an item I really wanted. Sometimes collecting is an endurance sport, which makes me wonder when the "sport" of collectibles will have its own collectibles.

Some auction houses offer a callback service. That means that if you're outbid, the house will call you back to see if you want to up your ante. Generally, this is done only on selective items, not the entire lot offered at an auction. I'm not a huge fan of callbacks for a couple of reasons. If you depend on them, you can easily relax your guard and sleep through the call. I know that from personal experience because that happened to me during one of my first auctions. I thought I was so savvy because I asked for a callback, but I wasn't savvy enough to stay awake. The callback came and went, as did an item I wanted desperately.

A less intrusive variation on the callback is when the auction house agrees to shoot you an email if you've been outbid. Easier on the ears and nerves than the old ringer.

BIDDING STRATEGIES

Let's look at some of the strategies I use when bidding. One approach I'll take is to look through a catalog, see what I'm interested in, and put it aside for a day or two. This is the same technique I'll use after compiling a "wish list." Let time become the selector. Then I'll pick the catalog up and if my interest has waned, I'll recycle the catalog. But if I'm still seriously drawn to an item, I'll often determine what my maximum bid will be. Then I'll place it.

At that point, all I have to do is wait to see if I'm the high bidder. Period. By bidding in that manner, I may scare away others from bidding at all. And by placing what I know is my highest bid, I'm not left having to constantly check the status of the bidding. Hey, I've given it my best shot. If I win, I win. If I don't, I don't.

Another tactic is to make sure I'm the high bidder before closing time, then call constantly during the extended period. I prefer to use the telephone for bidding, although when there is no thirty-minute rule (when the 10 p.m. deadline, for instance, is really 10 p.m.), I have lost out to computer generated "sniping." That's when bidders set up their computers to bid up to a point just before the closing time to make sure they post their bid at the last possible moment. When done successfully, sniping leaves no time for anyone else to bid before the bell, to borrow a term from boxing.

Auction houses often declare a "minimum bid" (MB). At first, you may be surprised by the relatively low MBs that you'll see. Auction houses, you see, have their own strategies, and theirs is designed to encourage as many people as possible to bid. They know that once you start bidding, you can become emotionally involved in the auction. In reality, the MB is usually set between 20 to 25 percent of what the house believes the winning bid will be. Some houses will offer an estimate of the winning bid in their catalogs, while others do not.

So let's say you've been successful in your first auction, but then find something about the object that alienates your affections. Beware, you may not return it, unless there are truly extenuating circumstances. In rare situations, for instance, the description in the catalog is flat-out wrong. That actually happened to me. I was the high bidder on what I thought was a game-used, signed Barry Bonds jersey. I received the uniform, but could not find Bonds' signature anywhere, and trust me, I looked everywhere.

I called the auction house and reported the problem. I

could tell they were a little skeptical, but they told me to send the jersey back to them so they could check for themselves.

I complied, and sure enough, they couldn't find Barry Bonds' John Hancock, either. That's when they told me I could have my money back or wait a few months until Bonds could sign the jersey during spring training. I chose to wait, and the jersey arrived in the spring freshly signed. If you find yourself in a similar situation, you must prove that the description of the items was wrong. In my case, that was pretty simple: no signature. The same situation prevailed with a collector friend of mine who bid successfully for what was reputed to be a team-signed ball of the 1960 Pittsburgh Pirates, but two very significant signatures were missing: Bill Mazeroski and Roberto Clemente, even though the description said their signatures were on the ball. Easily provable.

Far more daunting is when the catalog states that the condition of a signed ball is an "8," and you want to return it because you think it's just a "7." Good luck. You're not going to win that argument. Likewise, don't try to return a Greg Maddux-signed ball because you can't read his signature. The truth is, nobody can read Maddux's signature (see P. 74 for proof).

Before moving on, one final note about auctions: Even when an auction is labeled as Internet only, I've found that my telephone bids are accepted. A bid is a bid. See Page 198 for a list of auction houses that feature baseball auctions.

GARAGE SALES AND SWAP MEETS

When it comes to garage sales and swap meets, one overriding rule applies: get there early. If you're a night owl, this could be tough on you. And I should also tell you that it's not easy to find a real treasure at these events. But if you enjoy picking at garage sales and swap meets, you can find some real surprises. It helps tremendously to know what you're looking for. Remember my suggestions that you compile a "wish list" and keep it handy? That really helps when you're out at seven in the morning pouring through a table full of cards of baseball programs, staring at the 1966 Cincinnati Reds official roster, and you're not sure that's the year you wanted or the 1967 version. If you have your list handy, and it confirms that you've just found one of your personal Holy Grails, don't ask the price of the item. Ask how much the man or woman is asking for it. Signal that you're ready to bargain because nobody pays retail at these sales.

It's not unusual to find sports cards at garage sales and swap meets, and sometimes a huge box of them. If you know what you're doing, if you've done all the prep work, you could make a killing. Why? Because people selling their stuff at these events have, in effect, already signaled that they don't think their sports memorabilia is worth all that much. At the very least, it suggests that they haven't kept up to date on the value of their items. So if you come across Mickey Mantle's rookie card, pretend you're playing poker and you've just picked up your fourth ace. Ease into the negotiating, but don't blow the deal by nickel and diming. Get your card.

Garage sales and swap meets are often listed in local papers and online sites, but when you're out and about, look for those handmade announcements posted on poles and street signs. You can literally stumble upon great deals.

Likewise, when you're perusing online and print sites, keep in mind that some collectors advertise both their memorabilia and the items they're looking for. You can do that, too. It works both ways. *Sports Collectors Digest* is an effective vehicle for those kinds of solicitations. And keep in mind the handful of online sports websites, including collectorsuniverse.com, where you can trade—yes, *trade*—your items for memorabilia belonging to other collectors.

TRADE SHOWS AND CONVENTIONS

Two other really fun venues of note: trade shows and conventions. What's great about these events are the sheer number of participants and the vast variety of baseball items that are available. You don't even need to be in a buying mode to have fun and benefit from attending them. In fact, when you're first starting out, it's great to go to trade shows and conventions to get the big picture on sports collectibles. It can even help sharpen your own interest areas. There are lots of local trade shows, so you don't necessarily have to travel far to attend one. But if you like to travel, I heartily recommend the National Sports Collectors convention. It's a veritable gold mine for collectors and pickers, no matter their level of experience. For more information about this show, visit www.nsccshow.com.

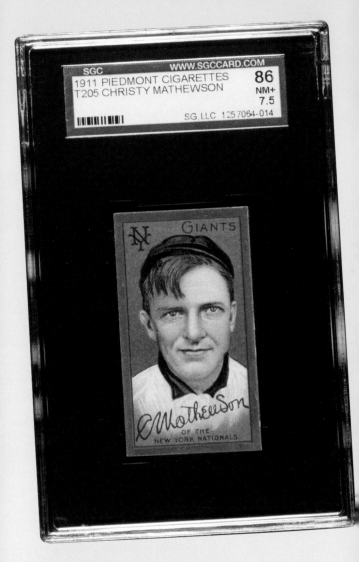

A 1911 T205 Piedmont Christy Mathewson SGC 86 NM+ 7.5. The inaugural class Hall of Fame pitcher is captured just near the apex of his storied career, and his face conveys the look of determination that would earn him a third place tie with G.C. Alexander on the career victories chart. Joining the most famous (Wagner, Cobb, Plank) and infamous (Merkle, Cicotte) ballplayers of the age, Mathewson stands as one of the key components from the comprehensive T205 card issue, **$7,767.50**.

Heritage Auctions

CHAPTER 2

Baseball Cards

Millions of us are veteran baseball card collectors, although most of us actually ended our "careers" before we hit our teens. Back then a lot of those cards smelled like bubble gum. I don't know about you, but I'd tear open a pack and pass on the pink stuff until I found out whether I'd lucked out with another favorite. In my case, it was Stan Musial. I was a diehard Cardinals fan and loved "Stan the Man."

As baseball cards have become part of American tradition and folklore, here's a brief history:

It was generally believed that baseball cards were first issued in 1887 by a few of the existing tobacco companies, but as the story about Bernice Gallego in Chapter 2 shows, she helped rewrite baseball card history with her discovery of the 1869 "Red Stocking B.B. Club of Cincinnati" card.

In 1887, a New York company, Goodwin & Company, issued the N172 series inside Old Judge and Gypsy Queen cigarette packs. More than 500 players are pictured, and as some players were pictured

Bowman color series 1953 baseball card, #32 Stan Musial, EX/MT 6 in a Beckett graded holder, **$200**.

Conestoga Auction Company

Fun Fact

In 1933, a chewing gum company, Goudey of Boston, included baseball cards with their chewing gum, the first time that idea had been implemented.

in several poses, nearly 3,500 different variations are known to exist. This set was issued between 1887-1890, as were other sets issued by other tobacco companies, notably Allen & Ginter. Cards issued in that time period were usually quite small, sometimes as small as 1-1/2 inch x 2-3/4 inches.

Not much happened on the baseball card front until the years 1909 to 1915. During that period, baseball cards became popular, and were issued by such diverse companies as tobacco, candy, and bread manufacturers, as well as sports magazines.

During this time, the American Tobacco Company issued the famous T206 set from 1909-1911. Of course, the Honus Wagner card, the jewel of baseball card collectors, is included in this set. Again, some players, such as Ty Cobb, are depicted on several cards with different poses. Other tobacco companies, such as Ramley, Hassan and Mecca, also issued cards, as did candy manufacturers such as American Caramel, Cracker Jack, and Zeenut Candy.

In most cases, the cards would be included with the product. One exception was the set of cards issued by *Sporting Life* magazine, which could only be ordered by mail.

During the 1930s, there were many card sets, primarily through gum companies. The Goudey Gum Company issued cards from 1933-1941, and the Bowman Gum Company issued the Play Ball sets in the late 1930s and early 1940s. During that time frame, and even as late as the 1960s, Exhibit cards were prominent, which were very distinctive in that they were thick, and black-and-white.

The 1932 U.S. Caramel Company issued a baseball set, which, if a person sent to the company the entire set, he would receive a free baseball or glove. It was not until the 1980s that card number 16 (Lindy Lindstrom) was discovered, and supposedly only two such cards are known to exist today.

Leaf, another gum company, issued a card set in 1948, and

A 1933 Goudey Big League Triple Babe Ruth uncut sheet. The 1933 Goudey Gum series of 240 was produced by the Boston-based Goudey Gum manufacturer in ten sheets containing 24 cards each, which were then cut, packaged with a stick of gum, and distributed. Naturally, Babe's famous face would grace what is now considered the first major gum card set of the 1930s. It sold at auction for **$131,450**.

Heritage Auctions

A 1933 Lou Gehrig Goudey card from the author's collection, **$1,200**.

Jeff Figler

This 1933 Babe Ruth Goudey card is also in the author's collection, **$5,500**.

Jeff Figler

Topps produced its first sets in 1951. Topps has been producing cards ever since. During the 1950s, the two major issuers of cards were Topps and Bowman. However, other companies such as Red Man Chewing Tobacco, Mother's Cookies, Wheaties cereal, Wilson Weiners, Esskay Meats, and Red Heart Dog Food, among many others, all issued cards. In 1955, the Topps Company bought out Bowman, and through 1980 dominated the card market. Other companies such as Post Cereal, Jello, Hostess, Kahn's Weiners, Milk Duds, and Hire's Root Beer issued cards, but did not match Topps' popularity. Finally, the Fleer Corporation slowly began to make a dent in the Topps domination.

Topps started producing baseball cards in 1952, and in the early 1950s staged some card battles with Bowman. After Topps bought out Bowman, it was the only company issuing Major League Baseball card sets from 1956 through 1980. It was quite successful in signing virtually every Major League player to an exclusive contract, and only companies promoting products such as cereal, meat products, and soda were able to fall outside the exclusive Topps agreement, and promote baseball cards. For the next couple of decades, manufacturers such as Fleer tried to get around the Topps agreement with players, but to no avail. Finally, after court decisions in 1980 and 1981, Fleer and Donruss could issue cards, but not with gum (Fleer issued cards with team logo stickers, and Donruss issued cards with puzzle pieces).

Topps has successfully produced variations of baseball cards, such as with special inserts, baseball coins, and posters. It has also been successful in distributing other sports cards, as well as sets of non-sports issues, such as of astronauts and presidents.

The Fleer Corporation started in 1914, and, ironically, in 1928 one of its employees Walter Diemer invented bubble gum. The first bubble gum was called Dubble Bubble. When it was first made, the only food coloring at the plant was pink, and therefore, at first, bubble gum was pink.

Through the years Fleer issued various types of cards, such as of movie stars, the Three Stooges, Hogan's Heroes, and football and basketball players. In 1959 it produced its first set of baseball cards, a Ted Williams set. Fleer was eventually bought out by Upper Deck.

1959 FLEER T. WILLIAMS   #29
JULY 21, 1946, TED   NM – MT 8
HITS FOR THE CYCLE
40362006

PSA

July 21, 1946, Ted Hits For The Cycle

A 1959 Fleer Ted Williams card, #29 PSA NM-MT 8, recounts the July 1946 summer day that saw him hit for the cycle against the St. Louis Browns. Slabbed within one of PSA's holders to ensure the condition it is in now, **$33**.

Heritage Auctions

Ted Williams signed 1959 Fleer card, PSA Authentic. The 1959 Ted Williams Fleer set is almost as famous as the great man himself. Card #63 of the set is perfectly signed neatly across the front in blue Sharpie, signature is bold and crisp, **$203.15**.

Heritage Auctions

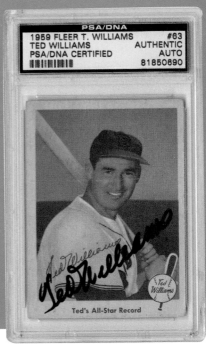

PSA/DNA

1959 FLEER T. WILLIAMS   #63
TED WILLIAMS   AUTHENTIC
PSA/DNA CERTIFIED   AUTO
81850690

Ted's All-Star Record

The Donruss Company started in 1958, and was named after its two owners, Don and Russ Wiener. Donruss also produced various types of sets of cards, based on television shows and musical groups, and in 1981 issued its first set of baseball cards. Eventually Donruss bought another card company, Score, but Donruss itself was bought by Panini America, a newcomer in American sports trading cards, in early 2009.

Upper Deck first started issuing cards in 1989. Its cards have been unique in that the Company included a hologram on the back of each one as a deterrent to counterfeiters. Even though the price of the Upper Deck cards has been higher than the price of its competitors' cards, Upper Deck cards are popular.

However, on August 6, 2009, Major League Baseball announced that it signed a multiyear exclusive arrangement with Topps. Surprisingly, in defiance of Major League Baseball's action, Upper Deck proceeded to issue sets in early 2010 which included logos and uniforms. Major League Baseball immediately sued Upper Deck in February of 2010, which resulted in a quick settlement a month later. Upper Deck agreed to pay a "substantial sum of monies" for unlicensed cards released. In addition, Upper Deck agreed to pay $2.4 million in license fees for 2009 cards.

Upper Deck and other companies still produce cards, but Topps is the only company that can use team names and logos. Major League Baseball justified its action as a way to bring order to the declining baseball card market.

Hopefully, it will. The number of card shops have declined

from about 5,000 in the U.S. in early 1990 to about 500 in 2011, along with a corresponding drop in revenue.

Let's see if the recent ruling will bring back the fun in collecting baseball cards. Maybe youngsters will start trading cards with their friends and building sets again. Now as far as putting cards on their bicycle spokes ... well, I doubt if that will ever happen again.

Oh, by the way, I am often asked how I started my collecting. Simple answer: My mother never threw away my baseball cards.

Collecting baseball cards is right up there with all things American. I must have opened hundreds of those bubble gum packs as a kid. Not just baseball, but football and basketball cards, too. I also got lucky because my mother held onto them for me. I know lots of men and women who have spent a good deal of time as adults just trying to reconstitute collections that got tossed by an overzealous parent intent on having a tidy garage, basement, or attic. I hope you're not one of them, but if you're wincing, you know better than I do how it feels to find years of collecting vanish overnight.

Those who have to rebuild childhood collections have one great advantage over their more youthful selves: baseball cards are easier to find and buy these days. There are small sports and hobby shops around the country—overseas, too—and, of course, it's often even easier to buy cards online. A good source for online cards is The Baseball Card Shop Online Store (baseballcardshop.net).

You can also trade cards online. The Web is a good way to find collectors who have just the cards you're interested in. Often, you can work out a deal that includes cash and cards, kind of like the front office of a pro team that trades a player and throws in some cash to sweeten the deal. You might even end up feeling like Brad Pitt in the movie, *Moneyball.*

Another great place to buy cards is at a local card show, where lots of vendors sell current, as well as vintage, cards. Those shows are usually held in metropolitan areas, but if you're not keeping an eye out for them, they can slip right under your radar screen. *Sports Collectors Digest* is a terrific source for listings of upcoming shows across the country.

Finding older cards can present real challenges. There are dealers who specialize not just in older 20th century cards, but those pricier gems from the 19th century as well. When it comes to cards, those much older ones are big game, so if you're hunting them, you'll definitely want to look at auction houses as well. A lot of those pricier cards end up at the more prominent houses.

But don't overlook eBay. After all, Bernice Gallegos started off trying to sell her Red Stockings card there. She got wise quickly, but other collectors have found great cards for low prices on that renowned online site.

I've mentioned the importance of writing a "wish list" of collectibles that you want. This is particularly true with cards because there may be dozens of them that you're on the lookout for. So keep that list handy, and keep in mind that persistence goes a long way in the card collecting game.

One aspect of card collecting that I especially enjoy is the "future's market": The rookie cards of players who might become superstars down the road. If you have a superstar's rookie card, you have a real value. As an example, one of the most valuable baseball cards of all time is Mickey Mantle's 1952 Topps #311 rookie card. It can be worth upward of $300,000. Now, that is truly an exceptional card, and it has to be in exceptional condition.

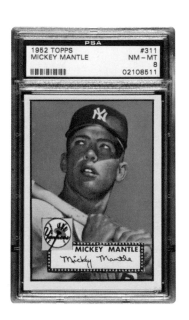

The image on this 1952 Topps Mickey Mantle card is an American icon, with the Mick posed in a right-handed batting stance, his eyes drifting up to the grandstand behind him, **$77,675**.

Heritage Auctions

A Guide to Grading Baseball Cards

It's fun for collectors to collect cards of their favorite players, teams, or cities. A big part of the fun is finding the best possible card. By that I mean cards that are well-centered with at least three sharp, square corners, and, of course, with no other flaws. There are several different grades of cards: Mint/Near Mint, Excellent, Very Good, Good, Fair, and Poor.

Keep in mind that there are also in-between grades such as VG-EX or even NRMT. It's also important to note that there are no precise price equivalents, but a "Good" card will be worth about half the value of a card in "Very Good" condition, and a "Fair" card will likely be worth roughly half the value of a "Good" card.

Then there are the exceptions to every rule. In this case, I'm referring to the Wagner and Mantle cards, which are extremely valuable no matter what condition they are in.

So where do you get your cards graded? Here are two suggestions: Sportscard Guaranty Corporation (SGC; www.sgccard.com), and Professional Sports Authenticator (PSA; www.psacard.com). Both firms charge to grade cards, but I've found that having a card evaluated increases its value enough to offset the cost of the grading.

A 1989 Gem Mint rookie card #548 of Ken Griffey, Jr. at the start of his Hall of Fame career, from the scarcer 1989 Fleer Glossy variant, graded PSA Gem Mint 10, **$1,673**.

Heritage Auctions

On the top of the heap, king of the hill, is the Near Mint/ Mint, or what some people will merely call Mint (MT). Again, there are no scientific measurements, but generally speaking, a Mint card's borders are in a ratio of no more than 65/35 side to side and top-to-bottom. Even if the pack of cards has just been opened, there can be imperfections. For a card to be Mint, there can't be any paper flaws, stains, and scratches, nothing of the kind. There has to be four sharp and square corners as well. If you think you have a perfect card, you probably don't. You may have a Near Mint card. The distinctions can be blurry. There could be three corners that are razor sharp, but the fourth might slightly dull. Possibly one of the borders might be a 75/25 side-to-side ratio. The card may look great, almost perfect, but it isn't. Your bubble may be burst, but don't worry, you've got a great card, especially if it's a Mantle, Griffey, or even a Pujols.

A 2001 Upper Deck Albert Pujols #295 BGS card, graded NM-MT+ 8.5. Don't tell Ted Williams, but there has been talk that this devastating Dominican slugger might just be the greatest hitter that ever lived. Now, it may be a bit too early to make such a pronouncement, but if he is one day remembered as such, you'll wish you had purchased this rookie card of the immensely talented player. Pujols absolutely ran away with the Rookie of the Year voting the year this #295 Upper Deck card appeared, **$47.**

Heritage Auctions

Excellent cards are quite common. In fact, among the grades of Excellent, Very Good, and Good, there is a real good chance that most of the baseball cards that are on this planet are in one of those categories. Excellent cards will still have corners that are pretty sharp. The cards will have some wear, but won't have any creases. However, they may have minor gum or wax stains.

A 1940 Play Ball Shoeless Joe Jackson #225, PSA EX 5. Shoeless Joe's banishment from the game following the 1920 season likewise signaled his departure from any and all card issues until the staff at Play Ball decided to give this superstar Black Sock a forgiving nod in 1940. The decision is certainly hailed by modern collectors, who assign a value to the number 225 card that far outpaces every other one in the set, **$1,553.50**.

Heritage Auctions

Very Good cards are usually distinguished by being well worn. Typically they are older cards that have just been around longer than most. Sound familiar? Unless a card has been well preserved, and kept in a climate-controlled environment, it is going to look its age. No, a little body lotion, anti-aging cream and hair color will not help baseball cards. And please, don't try trimming a card, as is what occurred with the Holy Grail T206 Wagner card (See P. 58-59). There are certain cardinal acts of misbehaving with cards, and doctoring a card is high on the taboo list. Do not trim (DNT).

A 1948 Leaf Joe DiMaggio #1, graded SGC 40 VG 3. This is one of the most coveted cards in the hobby, appealing to star card collectors, first-card-in-a-set collectors, pickers, and those with an eye for graphic design. This card displays obverse print ghosting, slight wrinkles to the cheap stock seen on the reverse and four corners that show only modest wear at tips, **$836.50.**

Heritage Auctions

A Good card is going to be similar in many ways to a Very Good card. They both have been around the block (yes, probably literally), and distinguishing them can be challenging. A Good card will probably have some well-defined creases, but the card can easily be read. It's not like you're going to confuse a Clete Boyer card with an Ernie Banks card. A Good card won't have any Scotch tape, thumbtack holes, or writing. There won't be any messages or secret codes.

A 1954 Topps Hall of Famer Rookie card of Ernie Banks #94, graded G, **$215.10**.

Heritage Auctions

A Fair card will show some damage, even thumbtack holes, tape, and possibly rubber band marks. There may have even been writing on the card, and it is likely that a little paper might be missing. The cardboard may be broken. It is not a real great card, but it is still all there.

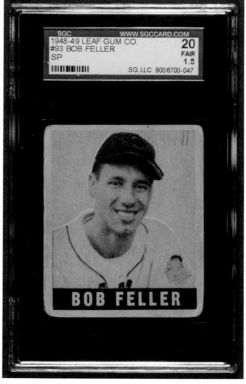

A 1948 Leaf card of Hall of Famer Bob Feller SP #93 graded SGC 20 Fair 1.5, has corner wear and an "11" pencil mark. This card was part of a gallery of ten 1948 Leaf Baseball cards with a subject roster exclusive to members of the Baseball Hall of Fame or a rare short-print, **$346.55**.

Heritage Auctions

• POOR

And then there are the Poor cards. Those Poor cards. Collectors and pickers will usually stay away from them, but of course there are exceptions, like with every rule. Poor cards usually have marks, and many have tape. Also, the DNT principle may have been violated. Of course, a picker would not pass on a Ruth or Mantle card in Poor condition. Oh, no. Those cards can still be sold for a nifty profit, and the chances are that the person selling a Poor card has already given up hope on it. Enter the picker. Of course there are stories of which dreams can be made. How about finding a T206 Honus Wagner in poor condition? It would be your lucky, day, week, month, year .... you get the idea. If you discovered a Poor Wagner card, it would not only make the evening news, but you would be a few hundred thousand dollars, or more, richer. To find out what one in much better condition is worth, turn the page.

Even in this Graded SCG 10 Poor 1 condition, this 1909-11 T206 Honus Wagner card is worth big bucks, since the Baseball Hall of Famer is best remembered today as the face on the most valuable and coveted of all baseball cards, no matter the condition, **$227,050**.

Heritage Auctions

The Holy Grail of Baseball Cards

Most collectors, and even non-collectors for that matter, are familiar with the "Holy Grail" of sports cards: the T206 Honus Wagner card. That one card has been the hope and dream of many collectors, the pinnacle of a baseball fan's journey, and to some the means to luxury. But through the years, the Wagner card has been the subject of a great deal of controversy.

Retracing history, Honus Wagner was an all-star shortstop for the Pittsburgh Pirates. He is regarded by many as being the premier player in the major leagues prior to the 1920s. Indeed, his highest achievement came in 1936 when the Baseball Writers Association of America selected him and Ty Cobb, Walter Johnson, Christy Mathewson, and Babe Ruth, for the Baseball Hall of Fame's inaugural induction.

From 1909 to 1911, the American Tobacco Company issued the T206 (the T was for tobacco) set of cards on two brands of cigarette boxes, Piedmont and Sweet Caporal. It is estimated that about 30 authentic Wagner cards exist today. There are two prevailing reasons for the scarcity of the card. The first theory is that Wagner requested that the production of his card be stopped because he did not want children to be influenced into buying tobacco products, since it was being used as a marketing tool. This theory has been disputed because Wagner himself was a smoker. The other theory is that he was not paid much by the tobacco company for the use of his image, and he requested that they stop production.

The fact remains that a minimal number of cards exist today, and the value of the scarce Wagner cards continues to escalate. In 1933, card collector Jefferson Burdick from Syracuse, New York, published *The American Card Catalog*, which was the first attempt to organize trading cards. Most cards were valued at less than $1, while the Wagner card was $50.

In 1985, Bill Mastro, a sports collectibles dealer, bought the only known Wagner card to be in mint condition in a private sale for $25,000. This card was later sold in 1987 to a West Coast collector Jim Copeland. Four years later, Copeland offered the card for auction on Sotheby's, and it was purchased for $451,000 by hockey star Wayne Gretzky, Los Angeles Kings' owner Bruce McNall, and actor John Candy. Later that year, recently formed Professional Sports Authenticator, Inc. (PSA) of Newport Beach, California, graded the card a "PSA NM-MT 8." The grading of this card set it apart, and from that time on, it has unquestionably been the most desirable trading card in the world.

In 1995, Gretzky sold his card to Walmart and Treat Entertainment for $500,000, to be used in a promotional contest. The contest was won by a Florida postal worker, Patricia Gibbs, who needed to sell it to pay the taxes on it. Christie's auctioned it for $640,000 to Michael Gidwitz of Chicago. In 2000, Gidwitz sold it on eBay to Brian Seigel for $1.265 million, and in 2007, Seigel sold it for $2.35 million. The card was then sold in April 2010 to Ken Kendrick, owner of the Arizona Diamondbacks, for $2.8 million, and when you add the buyer's commission the total price, it comes to about $3.1 million.

Naturally, the escalation of the one card, often called the Gretzky T206 Wagner card, has also raised the values of the other 30 or so Wagner cards, which are in a lesser condition.

The controversy surrounding the "Gretzky card" was whether it had been trimmed and "doctored," which to many card collectors is a vice. There had long been speculation that the pristine Wagner card was part of a T206 uncut sheet that landed in the hands of the party that sold that card, and the others from the sheet, to Mastro. Finally, Bill Mastro, under severe Federal scrutiny, admitted to trimming the card. If the cards were cut from a sheet, then they were not from the bottom of a cigarette box. Also, there are even rumors whether the PSA authenticators acted in good faith when they graded the card, as its policy is not to grade cards from sheets and cards that may have been altered.

Despite the controversy surrounding the card and how it came to be, the Wagner card is the "Holy Grail" of trading cards. For more about the card and the controversy, you might want to read the book, *The Card*, by Michael O'Keefe and Teri Thompson.

Card Packs

Card companies offer inserts in card packs, which have become popular. A pack might include pieces of a glove, bat, jersey, or other sports equipment. And I'm not exaggerating when I say "pieces." They literally cut up valuable collectibles and add them to the packs. What's the incentive for the card companies to cut up a baseball or bat and offer those surprising gems in the packs? They hope that the possibility of finding a valuable insert worth thousands of dollars is an inducement for collectors to buy more than one pack of cards. Think of it as the card collecting equivalent of the prize in a box of Cracker Jacks.

To the uninitiated, what I'm about to tell you may be surprising, but some collectors buy complete packs and *never open them.* That's right. In fact, unopened packs have become quite popular. It's the mystery that attracts people, and it harkens back to the "future's market" I mentioned. Every year, it seems at least one new star emerges in pro baseball and years from now, that player's "rookie" card could be worth hundreds, if not thousands of dollars. (Wondering why I just put "rookie" in quotes? Because sometimes determining a rookie card can be a challenge, since a player may have more than one first-year card.)

If an unopened pack contains a superstar's rookie card, and you have it in your pack, you could be sitting on a handsome profit. Clearly, it takes several years before your unopened pack will be worth much, but they're definitely worth saving. There are still some unopened packs of the T206 series (American Tobacco card series) from the early 20th century. They're extremely valuable because of the possibility that lurking in those cozy little confines is an undiscovered Honus Wagner card.

Some collectors try to get their cards signed by their favorite athletes. This can be a difficult task. Your best bet is to try to track down the ballplayers in spring training.

One of the most significant trading card finds in hobby history emerged from a small Ohio town, discovered in an attic in a box long forgotten. The pristine relics from the Dead Ball Era made their debut more than 100 years later – in 2012. Of the thirty players from the E98 series, the collection offered twenty-five players in two color variations, and a trio represented by a single background. The roster includes the greatest of the game: Ty Cobb, Honus Wagner, Chief Bender, Christy Mathewson, Connie Mack, Frank Chance, Hughie Jennings, Johnny Evers, Roger Bresnahan, Cy Young, plus others, **$286,800**.

Heritage Auctions

A 1941 Play Ball "Charley" Gehringer card, #19, SGC 88 NM/MT 8. Coming off a trip to the 1940 World Series where the Tigers came up one run short in losing to the Cincinnati Reds 2-1 in game 7, Gehringer continued to prove he was worthy of All-Star status. In his 17th year with Detroit, Gehringer hit .313 and scored 108 runs. A lifetime .320 hitter, Gehringer is still considered to be one of the best second basemen of all time, **$836.50**.

Heritage Auctions

A 1993 SP Derek Jeter, foil rookie #279 PSA Mint 9. Arguably Major League Baseball's most adored modern star, Jeter will one day be to current young baseball fans what Mickey Mantle is to a generation of baby boomers. This coveted rookie card will certainly grow in value as his 2014 retirement tour begins, **$1,434.**

Heritage Auctions

An unopened 1973 Topps Baseball Series 4 wax pack box with 24 uncirculated packs still contained inside the close to mint condition box they have called home since 1973. This series contains stars and HoFers Gaylord Perry, Willie McCovey, Juan Marichal, and Phil Niekro, plus various teams/coaches, along with the ever popular "All-Time Leader" cards, **$4,481.25.**

Heritage Auctions

A 1969 Reggie Jackson Oakland Athletics Topps rookie card #260, PSA 8 condition, **$338**.

Nate D. Sanders

Lot of 500 vintage baseball cards, 1952-1966, **$350**.

Saco River Auction

A 1971 Topps Hank Aaron #400 PSA Mint 9. The legendary Hall of Famer and (conditionally) dethroned Home Run King is the focus of this strong PSA Mint 9 example from the condition critical 1971 Topps series. This card has all the characteristics hobbyists desire of a high grade card and it features one of baseball's finest players, **$1,795.50**.

Heritage Auctions

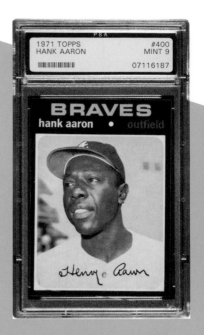

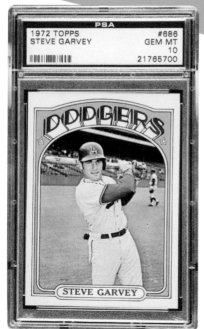

A 1972 Topps Steve Garvey #686 PSA Gem Mint 10, one of six examples (the top .06%) in Gem MT with none higher, **$2,270.50**.

Heritage Auctions

Two Topps Robert Clemente Baseball Cards, a 1956
Topps #33 and a 1957 Topps #76, **$98**.

Skinner, Inc.

A lot of 250 Topps baseball cards from 1964, **$225**.

Saco River Auction

Lot of 1984 Topps and 1989 Donruss cards, **$20**.

The Auction House Sacramento

Lot of two 1950 Bowman autographed baseball cards, #138 Allie Reynolds and #140 Pete Suder, both signed on the front in blue pen, overall condition VG-EX, **$40.**

Fusco Auctions

Lot of Tom Seaver baseball cards, various years and makers, **$20.**

Jaremos

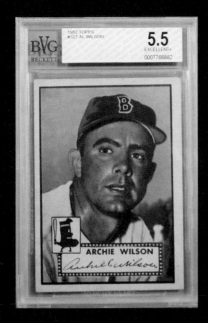

Topps 1952 series baseball card #327 Archie Wilson, EX+ 5.5 in a Beckett graded holder, **$130**.

Conestoga Auction Company

Bowman 1950 series baseball card #46 Yogi Berra, EX/MT+ 6.5, **$130**.

Conestoga Auction Company

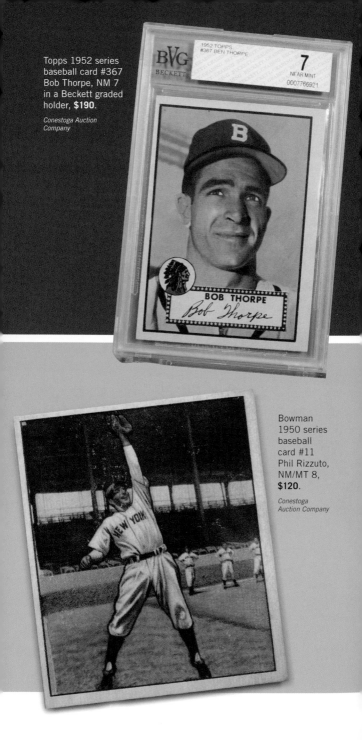

Topps 1952 series baseball card #367 Bob Thorpe, NM 7 in a Beckett graded holder, **$190**.

Conestoga Auction Company

Bowman 1950 series baseball card #11 Phil Rizzuto, NM/MT 8, **$120**.

Conestoga Auction Company

A 1975 Topps Robin Yount #223 rookie card, PSA Mint 9. The seventeenth man to join the illustrious 3,000 Hit Club, Yount played all twenty seasons of his first-ballot Hall of Fame career with the Milwaukee Brewers, **$896.25**.

Heritage Auctions

A 1984 O-Pee-Chee unopened wax pack, PSA Mint 9. Inside are potentially Gem MT examples of the rookie card of Don Mattingly, second year cards of Sandberg and Boggs, plus Brett, Henderson, Jackson, Strawberry, Schmidt, Ryan, Rose, Ripken and many other stars, **$50**.

Heritage Auctions

The Big Unit Randy Johnson's PSA Gem Mint 10 #25 rookie card from Upper Deck's vaunted 1989 debut issue. Johnson went on to become one of the more dominant hurlers at the big league level, **$191.20**.

Heritage Auctions

One of the many stars to emerge at baseball's top level as the 1980s came to a close, Sammy Sosa is shown here with this Gem Mint 10 rookie example from the 1990 Leaf issue, **$57.36**.

Heritage Auctions

A 1990 Leaf
Frank Thomas, a
slugger with the
Chicago White
Sox, #300 Gem
Mint PSA 10,
$66.92.

Heritage Auctions

Mike Piazza was
a star with the
Dodgers when
he burst onto the
scene in 1992.
Here is a pristine
Gem Mint 10
example of his
rookie card from
the 1992 Bowman
issue, **$95.60.**

Heritage Auctions

A 1984 Topps Tiffany Don Mattingly rookie card #8 SGC 98 Gem 10. Mattingly was one of the great players of the 1980s, **$262.90.**

Heritage Auctions

This is a Fleer Roger Clemens' best rookie card, graded a highly desirable PSA Mint 9, **$90.82.**

Heritage Auctions

A 1986 Topps All-Star card signed by Twins' icon Kirby Puckett. Signed in moderately bled blue Sharpie, this glossy exemplar exhibits NM-MT quality. LOA from JSA, **$65.**

Heritage Auctions

A 1993 classic Best Gold Barry Bonds #1 card graded GMA Gem M 10, **$20.**

Pioneer Auction Gallery

Greg Maddux isn't known for his signature being easy to read. Rawlings Official Major League Baseball, with MLB coa sticker, signed by Greg Maddux, for his 300th career win, in Plexiglas cube display, and Mounted Memories COA, **$90**.

Stephenson's Auctions

One of the best penmanships in baseball: Bob Gibson single-signed stat baseball. One of the most dominant eras ever enjoyed a pitcher is owned by dominant St. Louis Cardinals ace Bob Gibson. The hurler makes note of his numerous Hall of Fame credentials on four panels of this stat ball, with his perfect signature and induction date appearing on the sweet spot of the ONL (Coleman) orb, **$215.10**.

Heritage Auctions

CHAPTER 3

Baseballs

Signed baseballs have long reigned as one of the most popular of all collectibles. Other memorabilia—cards, photos, programs, tickets, equipment of all kinds—can be signed, but baseballs are beautiful to display. And they're relatively inexpensive to purchase, which is what you're going to have to do in most cases to get a signed ball. Think about it. Would you prefer to scamper after foul balls and home runs to try to get a ball for a player to sign, or simply buy one at a sporting goods store? Right. Me, too. But make sure you buy the right kind of baseball. It should be an official Major League ball manufactured by Rawlings. Any other brand will lessen the value of your ball, no matter who signs it. You'll find older signed baseballs from the official National League and American League, but that doesn't lessen the value of the ball because those were the ones used at that time.

While baseballs are relatively inexpensive to purchase, it's obtaining the signature that can be a challenge. Your best bet? Spring training, just like with cards. The players are more relaxed and accessible. Then there are the old standbys for

Three baseballs signed by Major League players Hank Aaron, Bob Feller and Minnie Minoso. Each in plastic displays, **$110**.
Leslie Hindman Auctioneers

tracking down signed baseballs—auctions, dealers, shows, and hobby shops.

Hopefully when you get a signed ball, you can read the signature. One of my pet peeves is professional athletes whose signatures are so illegible that even their bankers have trouble reading them. To cite just two examples: Greg Maddux and Mark McGwire. Man, we are talking chicken scratch. So let me give equal time for fine penmanship: Among the very best signatures are those of Tony Gwynn, Tom Glavine, and Bob Gibson.

SINGLE-SIGNED BALLS

It's one thing to have some ham-handed signature on a ball for yourself, but it's quite another thing to try to explain that to a child. I've known parents who went to great lengths to get a signed ball for their kids, only to find that Bozo the Clown could have whipped it out. There's really nothing you can do about that. It takes more gall than I've got to ask a busy athlete, who is already doing you a favor, to "slow down and sign it properly."

If you're buying a signed ball, that's a different story because you can always pass on making the purchase.

Let's look at the different types of signed balls, starting at the top—with the ones signed by presidents. Since the administration of William Howard Taft, presidents have been a part of baseball lore, and for good reason: Taft started two notable baseball traditions. Number one was throwing out the first pitch to start the Major League baseball season. The second tradition was the seventh inning stretch. Taft, a rather rotund sort, apparently couldn't remain seated for a full nine innings, so he started getting up and, well, stretching in the seventh—and we've all been doing it ever since.

But to true sports fans, baseballs signed by baseball players are the ones that are usually cherished most dearly. The ball that Mark McGwire of the St. Louis Cardinals slammed for his 70th home run in 1998 sold for $2.7 million. Phil Ozersky, a researcher at Washington University in St. Louis, was the lucky fan who came up with the ball. He used the proceeds to buy a few houses, and donated some of the money to various charities.

Hank Aaron's last homer, his 755th, was auctioned for $655,000 in 1999.

Another notable ball was one that barely made it out of the infield. Remember Mets Mookie Wilson's grounder that went through the legs of Boston Red Sox first baseman Bill Buckner during the 1986 World Series? That netted a cool $418,250.

A second infield wonder worth mentioning was the final out in the Red Sox/Angels 2004 World Series. A ground ball was slapped back to the Sox pitcher, Keith Foulke, who flipped the ball to the first sacker, Doug Mientkiewicz. Mientkiewicz did more than catch the ball—he held onto it, saying the ball would pay for four years of a college education. Regardless, the Red Sox wanted that ball to put on display. During the off-season, Mientkiewicz was traded to the New York Mets, for a Minor Leaguer,

Extremely tough Hall of Fame single-signed baseball by Freddie Lindstrom, signed by the legendary ball player in 7/10 black ballpoint, NM, presents "Hall of Fame 1976" neatly written on the side panel in an unknown hand, **$2,151**.

Heritage Auctions

no less. Finally, Mientkiewicz and the Red Sox reached an agreement that the team would get the ball at the end of the year.

For the fans, the rule of the jungle decides who catches or retrieves historic balls, and when a fan pockets such a ball, he or she also pockets a lot of money.

The ball that Barry Bonds hit for home run number 756, breaking Hank Aaron's record, was auctioned to Marc Ecko for $752,467. Later, Ecko generously donated it to the Baseball Hall of Fame—with an asterisk because Bonds was alleged to have used steroids.

But the story of Sal Durante lends real credence to the old expression, "Planning makes perfect." On October 1, 1961, Sal took his future bride to Yankee Stadium and bought tickets in section 33, box 163D in the lower right field stands, a primo spot to sit if you were looking to snag Roger Maris' 61st home run ball, which broke Babe Ruth's thirty-four-year-old record. Durante caught that homer barehanded and, in a magnificent gesture, offered the ball to Maris after the game—for *free!* It's hard to imagine anything like that happening nowadays. Now get this: Maris told Durante, "No, you keep the ball. Make yourself some money." *That* would probably never happen, either. You've got to love that era.

Eventually, Durante did sell the ball for $5,000 to a Sacramento restaurant owner. Maris met up with Durante when he delivered the prized ball, and gave the fan his lighter, as well as signing Durante's ticket stub to the historic game. The Yankees also gave Durante two season tickets for the 1962 season. As for that highly notable baseball, it eventually found its way to the Hall of Fame in Cooperstown.

While we're on the individual milestone beat, there's a ball that capped one of the most amazing single inning performances of all time. Some of you probably already know what I'm talking about. It happened on the night of April 23, 1999. That's when Fernando Tatis, the third baseman of the Cardinals, had a most memorable date with baseball history.

In the third inning of that Friday night game between the Redbirds and the Los Angeles Dodgers, Tatis smacked not just one grand slam home run, but two—*two*! In the same inning. It had never happened before, and it hasn't happened since.

Now, a fascinating footnote to Tatis's amazing feat was that Dodger pitcher Chan Ho Park surrendered BOTH grand slams.

St. Louis Cardinals Jersey #23, signed by Fernando Tatis. On April 23, 1999, Tatís made baseball history when he hit two grand slams in one inning against pitcher Chan Ho Park of the Los Angeles Dodgers, **$8,000**.

Jeff Figler

(How would you like to go down in the record books for that? No thanks.)

After the game, the man who caught the second grand slam ball exchanged it for the jersey Tatis wore that night, as well as the bat that produced the two round-trippers.

I felt so strongly about Tatis's magnificent accomplishment that I bought the bat and jersey for my museum.

TEAM BALLS

Now let's take a gander at team baseballs worthy of mention. The most valuable All-Star game ball is the one signed by the players of the 1933 All-Star game because it includes the autographs of luminaries Babe Ruth, Lou Gehrig, Jimmie Foxx, Joe Cronin, and others. But listen up. Even more valuable than that All-Star game ball is the one of the 1927 New York Yankees. You may have sniffed that one out already, especially if you knew the players on that amazing team. They included Ruth, Gehrig, and Tony Lazzeri. The manager was the legendary Miller Huggins. That's where the tricky part comes in. Huggins was sick most of the '27 season and did not manage the majority of the games. Therefore, the value of that team ball is greatly increased if his signature is on it. So what is the value? Anywhere from $10,000 to $60,000 and maybe more. Of course, the

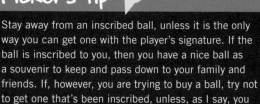

condition of the balls will dictate their value, but it's fair to say that any 1927 New York Yankees team-signed ball is a treasure. There just aren't many of them still around.

Many collectors try to obtain a team-signed ball for every year of a club's existence. Teams with a long history, such as the Chicago Cubs or the Boston Red Sox, pose a real challenge. It's easier with expansion teams like Minnesota, Houston, and the Mets.

One of the delights of collecting a team-signed ball every year is seeing which players remain on the team season after season. With an expansion team, you can complete this collection with minimum effort.

If you start buying balls, make sure to check if there's an inscription on it, such as "To Sally," or "For my friend, James." That takes away from the value of a ball as well. But sometimes an inscription on the ball may be the only way you'll get a signed ball from a particular player. The best example that comes to mind is the inestimable Jackie Robinson. A signed Robinson ball is tough to find, and one with an inscription may well be the only one within your price range.

Team-signed balls that have the signatures of Hall of Fame players on the "sweet spot"—the narrowest place between the two stitches—and also include the manager's autograph, are generally more valuable.

Sometimes you can come across a real bonanza—up to twenty or so team-signed balls from different years in a single collection that's up for sale. That's an easy way to acquire a handsome display.

Now, with most memorabilia—cards, bats, gloves, hats,

A 1953 Red Sox signed team ball, **$100**.

Saco River Auction

shoes, just about anything you can think of—you should have a player sign his name with a black or blue Sharpie pen. BUT NOT ON BASEBALLS. For the balls, you want them to use a ballpoint pen. Sharpies can "bleed" into the leather, eventually making the letters hard to read. You don't want to find yourself pointing to a ball in your display case and saying, "I know it looks like a mushroom, but I swear that's Derek Jeter's autograph."

Here's an interesting question: What's better, a baseball signed by a single superstar, or one that contains the star's autograph and the signatures of others? For the sake of discussion, let's say you're looking to buy a Babe Ruth signed ball. However, the ball you find also has a couple of other Yankees who were career journeymen. In that case, you'd prefer to have a Ruth only signed ball. But, if you happened on a ball signed by Ruth and Lou Gehrig, then there would be more value in having that ball than one signed by just one of those greats.

Gehrig signed a lot of baseballs, but Ruth was even more generous with his pen. And, as you may well know, both men died at relatively young ages. A few other superstars died young as well, which affected the quantity—and prices—of memorabilia that they signed. I'm thinking of Mel Ott, Christy Mathewson, and Roberto Clemente.

A goal that some collectors aim for is to have a signed ball by every member of the Baseball Hall of Fame. That's a tough one, but it is possible. Some of those autographed balls are so hard to track down that you might have to settle for the star's name on a team-signed ball. Still, as collections go, to have the signatures of every member of the HOF is quite an achievement.

Triple crown winners autographed baseball, signed by Ted Williams, Mickey Mantle, Carl Yastrzemski and Frank Robinson, **$600**.

Rago Arts and Auction Center

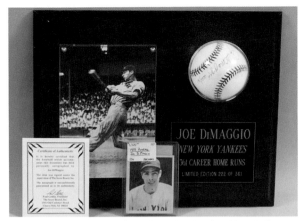

A 1939 Play Ball #26 Joe DiMaggio card and a signed baseball, the ball affixed to a plaque commemorating 361 home runs, limited edition 222 of 361. **$615**.

A 1940s Mel Ott-signed baseball, **$10,755**.

The finest Babe Ruth single-signed baseball known. Any great sports memorabilia collection should include a signed baseball. They aren't hard to find, partly because Ruth was among the first to see his autograph meant big money for his fans. Ruth's own granddaughter once admitted The Bambino would sign bats and balls all winter long and store them in a barn in preparation for "the busy season." He signed balls by the hundreds for the poor kids living around Yankee Stadium because he knew they were selling them to keep their family fed during the Great Depression. That said, collectors zero in on the best examples. This one is considered the finest Babe Ruth signed baseball known to exist, which helps explain why it brought a whopping **$388,375** at auction.

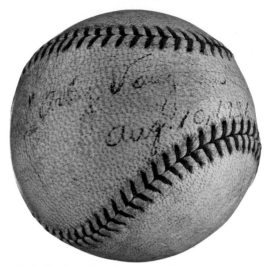

A 1936 Arky Vaughan single signed baseball. Just forty years old when he drowned during a 1952 fishing expedition, Vaughan as one of the greatest challenges to collectors of Hall of Fame singles ever since this Pittsburgh Pirates 1985 posthumous induction. The ball is autographed and dated ""Aug. 10, 1936" by Vaughan on the side panel at a level assessed as 3/10 in PSA/DNA's full grading letter of authenticity, **$4,790.76**.

Heritage Auctions

George Foster single-signed baseball. A five-time All-Star, Foster was a member of Cincinnati Reds Big Red Machine of the 1970s, leading the league in runs in 1977-78, **$12**.

Heritage Auctions

A 1940s Cy Young single-signed baseball, PSA NM 7, signed in black fountain pen, **$9,560**.

Heritage Auctions

A 1990 Nolan Ryan 300th Victory Game-used baseball. Just seven weeks after pitching the sixth no-hitter of his remarkable Hall of Fame career, the Major Leagues' career Strike Out King reached yet another milestone of baseball immortality, recording his 300th victory against the visiting Milwaukee Brewers. The presented OAL (Brown) ball saw action at the Texas Rangers' Arlington Stadium during the contest, a fact that Ryan notes on a side panel to the right of his 10/10 sweet spot signature. He writes, "Game Ball, 300th Win, 7/31/90," **$2,151**.

Heritage Auctions

Bo Jackson autographed baseball, with home plate stand and player's card, **$35**.

Bunte Auction Services, Inc.

Paul O'Neill 1998 game-used Young bat with COA, with signed
baseball included, **$350**.

Applebrook Auctions & Estate Sales

CHAPTER 4

Bats

There are four categories of collectible bats, and you'll want to know what they are before you ever step up to the plate:

- Game-used bat, which may even be cracked. Value is determined by who owned the bat and the size of the crack.
- A bat that has not been used in a game.
- A commemorative bat that honors a player, game, event, etc. These are desirable bats for display and are often autographed by players.
- A bat sold in a retail store.

If you start collecting or picking bats, here's a tip that isn't foul: Make sure you deal only with widely acknowledged experts. Why? It can be extremely difficult to know if a player actually used a particular bat during a game, even when the bat appears used. And there's a lot of money at stake with game-used bats.

Make friends with a bat expert. Take him to dinner. Pick up the check. It'll be cheaper in the long run if your bat expert has your back.

Bats That Could Beat Your Bank Account Senseless

- Cap Anson's 1888 game-used bat—$126,000
- Ty Cobb's 1925 game-used bat—nearly $75,000
- "Black Betsy" timber of Shoeless Joe Jackson—$577,610
- The 1923 bat that Babe Ruth used to swat the first home run in Yankee Stadium—are you ready for this?—$1.265 million.

While Jackie Robinson's 1947 bat is still missing, there are other game-used bats of his that have come to market over the years, including this 1949 All-Star Game-used one put up for auction by his family, **$83,650**.

Heritage Auctions

VALUABLE BAT WAITING TO BE FOUND

Let's go back to April 15, 1947, for the opening day of the baseball season between the Brooklyn Dodgers and the Cincinnati Reds. Do you remember why that was such an historic day? It was the career debut of a certain Brooklyn Dodgers first baseman, and not just any first sacker. Oh, no, the man we're talking about now would literally change the face of baseball and, quite arguably, of America itself: Jack "Jackie" Robinson.

Branch Rickey, the quotable Dodger general manager, had handpicked Robinson to cross the racial barrier in professional baseball. Robinson might not have been the best baseball player at the time, but Rickey trusted his temperament; Robinson was given explicit instructions to not fight back if he was abused physically or verbally. A lot to ask, but Robinson, it would turn out, had a spine made of steel.

So on that big day, Robinson made his long-awaited debut. He did not have a spectacular day with the bat, but even mentioning that does beg the question: Where is that bat that was used by the first African-American to play big league baseball? The answer is that no one knows because, clearly, no one cared to put it aside. The memorabilia craze had not arrived, and wouldn't for about two more decades, so nobody thought that the bat would be worth any more, or less, than any other bat. Robinson was not known to have asked for it, either.

Now, it's possible that racial prejudice was involved, but more than likely it was simply indifference. But fifty two years later, when Fernando Tatis of the St. Louis Cardinals belted two grand slams in one inning in a victory over the Los Angeles

Dodgers, you could bet your first-born that the batboy set that one aside. And I'm glad he did, because I was able to acquire it for my museum.

But here's what is so intriguing about the Robinson bat from that historic day: it could still be in someone's attic or garage. We could still be waiting for the bat's owner to come forward and surprise the world.

So what would that bat be worth? Easily a cool million, and maybe more.

Small grouping of baseball equipment, including four baseball bats, three painted, including a Hillerich & Bradsby No. 02 Crackerjack and a Joseph G. Kren Soft Ball No. 102, the two polychrome-painted unmarked, two small leather balls, and two mitts, a Reach and a J.C. Higgins, **$123**.

Skinner, Inc.

Red Sox's Trot Nixon-signed baseball bat, JSA COA, **$20**.

Saco River Auction

Oakland Athletic's Coco Crisp signed bat, JSA COA, **$30**.

Saco River Auction

Reggie Jackson signed bat, JSA COA, **$100**.

Saco River Auction

Ferguson Jenkins signed baseball bat, JSA COA, **$30**.

Saco River Auction

Johnny Mize signed baseball bat, **$50**.

Saco River Auction

Genuine Louisville Slugger baseball bat P72, signed by Derek Jeter, in oak and Plexiglas display, COA by Steiner, **$500**.

Stephenson's Auctions

Genuine Louisville Slugger Baseball Bat C271, signed by Ken Griffey, Jr., in oak and Plexiglas display, numbered 9/10, COA, BAG 35966, **$180**.

Stephenson's Auctions

Three vintage bats: One says Wharton College, one is a Winner bat and the last one is a Gil Hodges bat. Some cracking, all have been fairly well used. Wharton bat is Mickey Mantle Model, condition Good to Very Good, largest bat is 35" long, **$20**.

Dan Morphy Auctions LLC

Tony Gwynn Hit #2,998 game-used uniform, cap, helmet, cleats, bat and baseball from 1999. He's one of the most skilled batsmen in the game's long history and the only man on the top twenty list for career batting average that did not play before the Second World War. With this uniform and equipment, Gwynn moved within two steps of the elite 3,000 Hit Club and assured baseball immortality. Package includes: 1) Road blue jersey and matching gray pants, jersey sports "Padres 19" on chest with "Gwynn 19" on verso, thirtieth anniversary team patch on left sleeve, "Russell Athletic Diamond Collection [size] 50" label in tail, with "100% Polyester" flap tag; 2) Cap with "19" in black marker inside dome and "New Era [size] 7-1/8" tagging; 3) Batting helmet with "American Baseball Cap [size] 7-1/8" label inside is notated for the event on label and interior padding; 4) Batting gloves and wristbands; 5) Cleats are Nike size 11; 6) Signature model Louisville Slugger B267 with handwritten notations on knob address all relevant information about style, length, weight and jersey number: "B267c, 33-30.5, 19," signed in bold black Sharpie on barrel with "#2998" notation; 7) Baseball, the ONL (Coleman) sphere is the very one that recorded this historic hit, notated with date and hit total, unsigned, **$6,572.50**.

Heritage Auctions

CHAPTER 5

Equipment

It's possible for a picker to acquire a significant amount of equipment used by a particular player.

BATTING HELMETS AND CAPS

Let's start at the top with batting helmets and caps. They are definitely available, and what may be most surprising is that they're generally affordable. I'm talking about game-used helmets, of course. Signed caps can be pricey, but only if the autograph comes from a star player.

Group of early baseball items, lot includes seven gloves, one ball, two masks and an umpire's chest protector and mask, all in good or better condition, **$325**.

Lang's Auction

A signed batting helmet from Alex Rodriguez sold for about $360, while a Ken Griffey Jr. signed batting helmet went for about $300 more at $660.

Best place to find helmets and caps? Catalog auctions and eBay.

BATTING GLOVES

Moving south on the player's anatomy, your favorite player's battling gloves are also waiting to be scooped up. Some are even signed. Ditto when we drop down to his cleats (grass stains and infield grime come at no extra charge). A pair of Derek Jeter's went for almost $600. A Sammy Sosa game-used batting glove fetched $227.

OTHER GLOVES

It's safe to say that gloves are not quite as popular with collectors as other pieces of equipment, like balls and bats, but gloves do have their fans—maybe because they can bring back a lot of memories to a collector, many of whom still own their earliest gloves.

In the 1920s, manufacturers began putting players' names on gloves, which increased their appeal and, predictably

The perfect complement to a Ruth-signed ball is one of his game-worn New York Yankee caps. This cap dates to 1932, the year he called the shot during the fifth inning of Game 3 of the World Series. Ruth was quite the showman and his penchant for antics on the field filled seats like few others could. His cap sold for **$200,000** at auction.

Heritage Auctions

Grouping of baseball equipment including vintage gloves, miscellaneous baseballs and jerseys, catcher's gear, and cleats, **$861**.

Skinner, Inc.

enough, their value. I'll give you a good example: A G41 Draper Maynard Babe Ruth. That glove can easily fetch thousands, a price that illustrates that the more vintage a glove, the more value it holds.

Fingerless baseball gloves from the 1870s and 1880s also fetch upwards of ten grand.

Gloves usually appeal more to advanced collectors, perhaps because the prices can be so daunting.

Circa 1970s collection of professional model baseball caps, rare styles, lot of 9. New Era and Wilson hats are featured in this compilation of professional model game caps. Each of these originates from the personal collection of Patrick McBride, a Milwaukee Brewers batboy in the 1970's. According to McBride, he was given these hats to wear as the visiting team's batboy. Most are void of numbers, but those which feature one will be noted. Included are the following rarely encountered styles. 1.) mid-to-late '60s White Sox, size 7-3/8" blue cap with a cardboard Wilson insert; 2.) 1971-75 White Sox size 7-1/2" red cap, a leather headband is secured on the inside; 3.) '70s Orioles size 7-3/8" cap, wear is visible on the headband; 4.) 1970-71 Cleveland Indians Wilson size 7-1/4" cap with "42" written on the underside; Dick Elsworth wore that number in 1970; 5.) circa 1970s Twins size 7-1/2" with "33" and the size written in vintage marker; 6.) Yankees "Pro KM size 7-3/8" cap with "24" written on the underside; Al Downing wore the number from 1961-69; 7.) A 1971 Angels one-year style Pro KM size 7-1/2" cap which appears unused, rare one-year style; 8.) 1970s Royals heavily used size 7-1/4" cap, an indecipherable number is visible under the brim; 9.) 1970s Oakland As Pro KM size 7-1/2" cap, no player identified, **$956**.

Heritage Auctions

Two-time American League MVP Frank Thomas autographed Chicago White Sox baseball helmet, signed "Frank Thomas 35," 9" h x 9" w x 12" d, **$200**.

Great Gatsby's Antiques and Auctions

A 2012 Albert Pujols signed Angels cap. The supreme slugger signed this size 7" cap in bold black Sharpie on front, authentication is secured with a PSA/DNA sticker and matching certificate, LOA from PSA/DNA, **$179.25**.

Heritage Auctions

An Andy Benes cap, worn on Arizona Diamondbacks' opening-day game in 1998, exhibiting nice wear throughout, this size 8" cap features an "Opening Day March 31, 1998" patch on the side, No. 40 marked under the brim, **$221.08**.

Heritage Auctions

The Ichiro Suzuki batting helmet he wore in 2007 as he drilled his 1,500th Major League hit in a 14-10 Seattle victory over the visiting Oakland As, size 7-5/8 "Rawlings." It took the Japanese superstar 1,060 games to reach the mark, outpacing every player in history other than Al Simmons and George Sisler. The helmet exhibits a single game's wear and bears an MLB holographic authentication sticker on verso confirming its implementation in Ichiro history, **$4,780**.

Heritage Auctions

Los Angeles Dodgers baseball helmet signed by Edwin "Duke" Snider, a Hall of Famer who was once one of the kings of New York when it came to talkin' baseball in the 1950s. Snider hit 407 home runs during his 18-year big-league career with the Dodgers, Mets and Giants. He played 16 seasons for the Dodgers, making his debut for Brooklyn in 1947. He powered the Dodgers to their only World Series crown in Brooklyn in 1955, a year in which he hit 42 home runs and drove in a league-leading 136 RBIs, before making the move to Los Angeles where he helped win another Series in 1959. PSA certified, excellent condition, certificate of authenticity included, **$250**.

Seized Assets Auctioneers

Frank Robinson signed Baltimore Orioles authentic helmet. Baltimore's finest slugger signed this in gold paint pen, a PSA/DNA sticker and matching certificate included, **$78**.

Heritage Auctions

New York Mets batting helmet signed by superstar David Wright, signed on the brim in pristine silver Sharpie, size 7-3/8", **$248.56**.

Heritage Auctions

Darren Daulton signed catcher's mask, used in the 1990s, the "All-Star FMSLW 25 EXT PRO" gear is signed on the back in bold Sharpie by the former Phillies notable, **$125.48**.

Heritage Auctions

This is one of just a few known surviving catcher's masks worn by Hall of Famer backstop Yogi Berra during his Yankees tenure. Catcher's gear from this iconic Yankee is the toughest of quarry for the Yankee collector, **$16,730**.

Heritage Auctions

A 2006 Paul Lo Duca game-worn New York Mets catcher's mask, accompanied with an LOA from Steiner marked "Rawlings LWMX," **$167.30**.

Heritage Auctions

Vintage goggle-eyed catcher's mask remains in great shape despite it most likely dating from the 1920s, all original padding and leather remains present, but much of it has started to crack, strap is original and remains fully attached to the mask, manufacturer's logo in found on the front of the chin pad, may have been used as early as 1910 and as late as the mid-1930s, about 8" x 10", **$448.13**.

Heritage Auctions

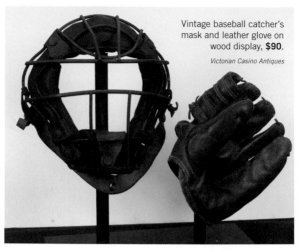

Vintage baseball catcher's mask and leather glove on wood display, **$90**.

Victorian Casino Antiques

A 2000's Mike Piazza game-used catcher's mitt. The Steroid Era has made Hall of Fame enshrinement a tough prospect for anybody who played during those years, so while Piazza's name has not been one most commonly associated with PED's, it's clearly the only thing that has kept him out of Cooperstown thus far. Yellow "Mike Piazza" embroidered on thumb, **$717**.

Heritage Auctions

"Rawlings, The Gold Glove Co." black leather glove signed by HOFer Ozzie Smith, The Wizard added a "13 X Gold Glove" inscription to this, which exhibits Mint quality throughout, **$298.75**.

Heritage Auctions

A 1966 Sandy Koufax game-worn fielder's glove, a moderately age-faded number "32" appears at the thumb, with an even paler "Koo-Foo" (Koufax's nickname around the Dodgers' clubhouse) marked at the pinky finger, handwritten inscription to umpire Doug Harvey, "To Doug, Very Best Wishes, Sandy Koufax," **$107,550**.

Heritage Auctions

A 2013 Mariano Rivera game-used fielder's glove. Having announced his intention to retire at the end of the 2013 season before spring training had even begun, Rivera exhibited his characteristic generosity with the ordering of dozens of fielder's gloves which he intended to wear for a single game and then donate to worthy causes or individuals. This is one of those gloves. The soft black leather Nike Diamond Elite model is embroidered with "Mariano Rivera, Phil 4:13" at the thumb, the Bible verse referenced being, "I can do all things through Him who gives me strength," on the outside fingers, Rivera signs in 9/10 silver Sharpie adding his jersey number and the words, "Game Used 2013 Season," **$10,157.50**.

Heritage Auctions

A Pete Rose game-used Cincinnati Reds jersey from 1978, one of the most significant years of his career and one populated by his entry into the 3,000 Hit Club, his memorable forty-four game hitting streak, and the post-season granting of free agency and subsequent signing by the Phillies. "Cincinnati 14" on the chest, with "Rose 14" on verso, interior collar holds "Wilson [size] 44" label, swatch at lower left front tail is embroidered "78 1," with a faded "Purchased from Cincinnati Reds" stamp just below, **$6.572.50**.

Heritage Auctions

CHAPTER 6

Jerseys and Uniforms

When collectors talk about acquiring uniforms, what they're generally referring to are jerseys, and they come in three categories, so let's clarify what they are before we delve into this realm any deeper:

- The "game" jersey: This refers to a jersey that is not worn by a player during a game.
- "Game worn": This is a jersey worn during a game in which the player never took the field. That could be a pitcher, for example, who wore the jersey, but never took the mound.
- "Game used": This, as you may surmise, refers to a jersey that is worn by a player who sees action in a game. A game-used jersey is the most valuable of the three types to collectors, and the ones pickers should be looking for.

This is the jersey Lou Gehrig was wearing when the Yankees dominated in 1927. With a batting order called Murderer's Row for obvious reasons, the team delivered the most devastating three-four punch for its historical context that the game has ever seen. Ruth's sixty circuits in 1927 were trailed by Gehrig's forty-seven. In fact, the duo of Ruth and Gehrig produced more than twice the home run output of every nearly every other American League team, **$717,000**.

Heritage Auctions

Jerseys are widely available, but be forewarned that they can be expensive, none more so than the $4,415,658 paid for Babe Ruth's 1920 uniform top, the earliest one known to have been worn by the Bambino. The more than $4.4 million jersey sold by SCP Auctions in 2012 was a record for sports memorabilia of all kinds, even topping James Naismith's *Founding Rules of Basketball*, which sold for a little more than $4.3 million. The Babe reigns supreme once more. Another Ruth jersey sold for $657,250. That almost seems like a bargain.

While other athletes' jerseys don't come close to that $4.4 million price tag, they are by no means inexpensive. Jackie Robinson's game-used jersey sold for $341,779. A 1928 Ty Cobb signed Philadelphia jersey cost almost as much at $332,500, although that's another bargain compared to the one shown below. Sandy Koufax's 1965 LA Dodger home jersey brought in $262,900.

More affordable jerseys—though by no means cheap—include Bob Gibson's at $60,667 and Ken Griffey's for $11,625.

Babe Ruth's #3 New York Yankees jersey remains a shining symbol of pre-war Americana. When he wore this jersey during Major League Baseball's very first 1933 All-Star Game, it marked the beginning of his slide into retirement and his struggle with weight, but the year was still a career standout as he batted .301, with 34 home runs, 103 RBIs, and a league-leading 114 walks. His jersey sold for a whopping **$657,250**.

Heritage Auctions

A signed jersey by some of the Boston Red Sox all-time greats including Fred Lynn, Dwight Evans, Johnny Pesky, and more, **$225**.

Saco River Auction

Tony Gwynn and Stan Musial jerseys and *Sporting News* cover, featuring both of them, and commemorating Gwynn's 3,000th hit, **$83,000**.

Jeff Figler

A Top 10 moment in a legendary career! The Derek Jeter first (and only) Grand Slam game-used 2005 jersey of the New York Yankee. It was the 136th time in his career that the Yankee captain had stridden to the plate with the bases loaded, on June 18, 2005. His past production in this scenario had been impressive by any reasonable standard--forty-five for 135, a solid .333 average, with 114 runs driven in. But none of those RBIs had ever come in a grouping of four. With 155 career homers to his name, the superstar shortstop held the record both for active players and Yankee franchise history as the greatest long ball tally without a grand slam among them. A two-and-one delivery in the bottom of the sixth from Chicago Cubs right-hander Joe Borowski would prove to be the drought-breaker, a blast over the left-center field wall to break the interleague game wide open. The living legend inscribed the chest in 10/10 blue Sharpie, "Derek Jeter, 1st Grand Slam, 6-18-05, Yankees 8 Cubs 1." A second blue Sharpie autograph appears on verso as well. Jeter will go down in history as one of the all-time Yankee greats, **$41,825.**

Heritage Auctions

Bob Gibson game-used jersey, **$60,667**.

Jeff Figler

An autographed #3 Edgar Renteria with flag over name on back
(September 2001), Dave Duncan #18, autographed #3 Dave Rickets
with 1987 World Series patch, and a 1997 Jackie Robinson Day with
arm patch and 4 on back, all button up with the birds on the bat logo
across chest, **$550**.

Ivey-Selkirk Auctioneer

Lot of two Stephen Strasburg Washington Nationals signed baseball
jerseys, both with certificates of authenticity, **$130**.

Scott Grasso

An exceedingly rare full uniform worn by Hall of Famer George Brett during the historic American League MVP 1980 season when he finished at .390, the second-highest average (after Tony Gwynn's strike-season .394). The classic powder blue road-style will forever be linked to Brett, the block-lettered "Kansas City" arching across the chest, team logo patch affixed to left sleeve, with "Brett 5" decorating the back. Matching pants are tagged "Wilson" inside the waistband, with the size a hand-embroidered "33." Just to the left is an embroidered swatch announcing "5 80 25," indicating jersey number, year and inseam. Both jersey and pants exhibit fine season-long wear with apparent tobacco juice spotting and fabric abrasions from fielding and base-running acrobatics, **$9,560**.

Heritage Auctions

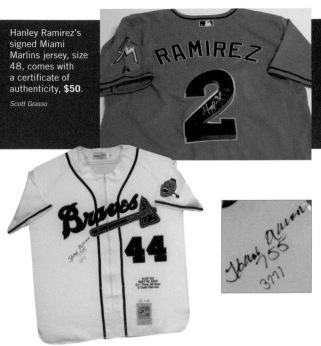

Hanley Ramirez's signed Miami Marlins jersey, size 48, comes with a certificate of authenticity, **$50**.

Scott Grasso

Framed Cooperstown Collection Atlanta Braves jersey, Mitchell and Ness #44, signed by Hank Aaron with 755 and 3771, Major League Baseball authenticated #MT00022228, limited edition 12/50, HOF 1957 NL MVP, 21- time All Star, 3 Gold Gloves, frame size 38" x 38", **$400**.

Stephenson's Auction

Lot of five signed jerseys by baseball greats Brooks Robinson, Bob Gibson, Johnny Bench, Ozzie Smith and Tommy Lasorda, each includes a PSA/DNA sticker and matching certificate for authentication, **$489.95**.

Heritage Auctions

Roger Maris white base bobbing head doll, 1961-63. The highly coveted Maris doll is in excellent condition, save only for a 1/4-inch square chip underneath the bill of the cap and a homemade "9" penned on his shirt back with the same instrument used to fill in the pinstripes, **$657.25.**

Heritage Auctions

CHAPTER 7

Bobbing Head Dolls and Statues

STATUES

Hartland Plastics, Inc. is the biggest name in sports statues. The company issued its first baseball statues, or figurines as they're commonly called, early in 1958. But, as noted earlier, the company really made its mark in the early 1960s when it released its first set of nine National League players, nine American League players, a minor leaguer, and a batboy. Those are the most desirable statues among collectors.

Hartland re-issued its famous sets

Sandy Koufax signed Salvino figurine, the limited-edition figure comes complete with certificate of authenticity and the original box it was issued in, **$450**.

New York Times Store

twenty-five years later, featuring some of the same players. It was immediately popular, and less expensive to boot.

Salvino and Gartland are two other companies that have issued figurines, and autographed statues as well.

Most statues range in price from $50 to several hundred dollars. The exception is the Dick Groat Hartland statue I mention in the introduction, which can be worth as much as $3,000, if it's in perfect condition. And, as also noted earlier, if you get Groat's signature on it, the price tag could easily jump to $6,000.

I'm an enthusiastic collector of Hartland figurines, and I've found that auctions are often the best way to track down the ones you want. And if you don't find what you want at the auction houses, jump right online or hit the trade shows. You'll find them.

BOBBING HEAD DOLLS

Most collectors are familiar with bobbing head dolls (aka bobblehead dolls and nodders). They're kind of goofy looking, highly collectible, and can be valuable. Lots of them are given away as promotional items at sporting events. Get this: I went to a baseball game in Phoenix where they were giving away bobbing head dolls of a player who'd been traded a couple of weeks earlier. Some players get no respect.

Bobbing head dolls came into prominence in

Ricky Henderson bobbing head doll, **$65**.

Jeff Figler

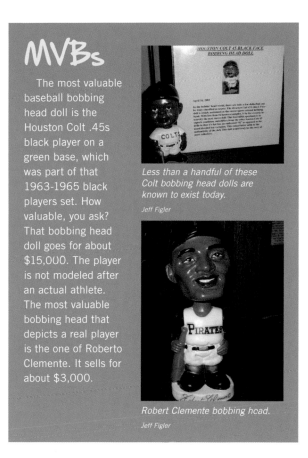

MVBs

The most valuable baseball bobbing head doll is the Houston Colt .45s black player on a green base, which was part of that 1963-1965 black players set. How valuable, you ask? That bobbing head doll goes for about $15,000. The player is not modeled after an actual athlete. The most valuable bobbing head that depicts a real player is the one of Roberto Clemente. It sells for about $3,000.

Less than a handful of these Colt bobbing head dolls are known to exist today.

Jeff Figler

Robert Clemente bobbing head.

Jeff Figler

1960, when the first baseball set appeared, which was the 1960-1961 square color base set with bobbing head dolls representing different teams. They're colorful in their tiny uniforms. The rarest doll in that set is the Washington Senators doll, which has a dark blue base. Other sets of note in the 1960s included the 1961-1962 white base miniatures, the 1961-1963 white base set, the 1963-1965 black player set, the 1963-1965 green base set, and the 1966-1971 gold base set.

There are several baseball sets. You need to collect them with care, if your goal is to obtain a complete set. Frankly, sometimes it's easier to collect bobbing head dolls by team, rather than by the established sets.

Don't rush to buy a bobbing head doll when one catches your eye. Yes, they're cuter than kittens. And, yes, they display nicely, are lightweight, and easy to move. But before you buy a bobbing, you should inspect it carefully. Here's why: Bobbing heads are sometimes damaged around their necks and ankles; therefore, you want to check those areas carefully to see if the doll has been broken and glued together, and whether the original paint is still intact. Also, check the rear of the doll because frequently that's where you'll find chipping. And always look inside the doll's head for cracks. Some dolls won't show a crack because they've been repainted on the outside. That's why it's always a good idea to take a close look at the inside of that tiny little skull; a cracked doll is worth only about 10 percent of a non-cracked doll.

Clearly, the dolls are fragile, so much so that collectors will often wrap tissue around their necks to keep them from snapping.

But man, are they darling.

Display of entire original set of Hartland statues, along with batboy and minor leaguer, **$3,500-$4,000**.

Jeff Figler

Babe Ruth Hartland statue with signed baseball with and card, **$250**.

Jeff Figler

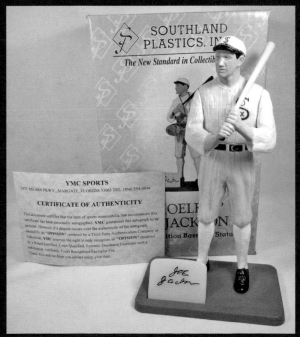

Limited edition Shoeless Joe Jackson statue, approximately 9" high,
$50.

Pioneer Auction Gallery

Two plastic Hartland statues, Ed Mathews and Warren Spahn, some yellowing, original issues, C6, **$60.**

Lloyd Ralston Gallery

Mickey Mantle white base bobbing head doll, 1961-63, minor wear, small loss of paint visible at the underside of Yankees cap, **$537.75.**

Heritage Auctions

Lot of two bobbing head dolls: Oakland Athletics, TEI, China, circa 1990, 8" high; and San Francisco Giants, 6" high, both in excellent condition, **$100**.

Victorian Casino Antiques

New York Yankees white base bobbing head with original box, 1961-63, only one hairline crack in the back of the head and moderate wear, **$203.15**.

Heritage Auctions

New York Yankees green base bobbing head, 1963-65, highly collectible, some chipping at interior of head where skull meets neck is only visible upon close inspection, otherwise no visual distractions of note, **$288**.

Heritage Auctions

St. Louis Cardinals mascot bobbing heads, **$272.50.**

Jeff Figler

A 1949 Brooklyn Dodgers Ho Jo the Bum latex plastic squeaky mascot toy manufactured by Rempel Mfg of Akron, Ohio, designed by Fred G. Reinert, original patina, minor loss to paint throughout, squeaker still works, 4" x 2" x 6", **$90.**

MG Neely Auction

Baltimore Orioles gold base bobbing head doll, 1966-71, paint remains vibrant on this example, which rates a true Mint, **$155.35.**

Heritage Auctions

Atlanta Braves bobbing head with gold round base, made in Japan, box with cardboard insert, some slight chipping and wear, condition Very Good to Excellent, 7" high, **$100**.

Dan Morphy Auctions LLC.

Cleveland Indians Chief Wahoo bobbing head, round green base, with original box, 1960s, EX condition with just a small paint chip to the feather and back of the head, no cracks or repairs, marked Made in Japan and stamped 1962 on the bottom of the base, comes with original "My Favorite Baseball Team" box, approximately 7-1/4" high, **$160**.

Fusco Auctions

This Cleveland Indians mascot piece was issued circa 1940s, and is a 6-1/2" rarity. It sold for **$54** at auction.

Heritage Auctions

Detroit Tigers gold base bobbing head, 1967-72, couple of minor hairlines under the chin, **$69**.

Heritage Auctions

WHITE SOX

JOE JACKSON

A 1916 BF2 Ferguson Bakery felt pennant featuring Joe Jackson. This series of almost 100 subjects was circulated by Ferguson Bakeries on a limited basis. Each six-inch pennant-shaped piece of felt features a small black and white photo of the designated player glued down surrounded by the players name and team. One of the key names of the series is this man, Shoeless Joe Jackson. In 1916, his first year with the White Sox, he was still at the top of his game and this BF2 pennant is one of his more scarce collectibles, near mint condition, **$1,912.**

Heritage Auctions

CHAPTER 8

Pennants and Pins

Pennants have gained a great deal of popularity over the years. Many collectors appreciate the nostalgic qualities of pennants. Pennants from the early days of baseball were made from a soft felt material that I think is far superior to the fabric used in contemporary pennants. Team logos were often painted on the earlier pennants.

More recent pennants are usually made from synthetic materials, and the logos are silk screened onto them. Since 1969, the Major League Baseball logo has appeared on all pennants.

The most valuable pennants are, of course, rare, and thus quite costly. The priciest is probably a 1919 Chicago White Sox pennant that was auctioned for $34,500. Nothing to sneeze at .... or on.

The 1922 New York Yankees American League Championship pennant, which includes the portraits of players' heads, including the redoubtable Babe Ruth, can go for $25,000.

From the same year, a 1922 New York Giants National League Championship pennant can run you about $7,000.

Oversized pennants, issued in the early 20th century, are valued at upward of $3,000.

Philadelphia Athletics felt pennant, 11-1/2", **$45**.

Hassinger & Courtney Auctioneering

Condition is always a factor, but a famous player's name on pennant will also drive up the price.

A good place to look for pennants is on eBay, where you can often pick up rare ones for a few hundred dollars.

Like bobbing head dolls, pennants are colorful, lightweight, easy, and fun to display.

PINS

Team pins and press pins are ideal collectibles because they're small, lightweight, and sometimes quite colorful. And for the most part, they're affordable, but not always. Distributed to the media, press pins quickly gain wider circulation and because they've been around since 1910, some rare press pins can prove costly. The original 1911 Philadelphia As press pins have sold for more than $20,000. A 1922 New York Yankees World Series press pin went for $5,758, and a 1917 Chicago White Sox pin fetched $5,500.

But take heart because most of the time you can find more common press pins for about $50.

The brown, white and gold cap form lapel pin, from the collection of Bob Ingham, first sports director for KSD TV, and former employee of KMOX, **$550**.

Ivey-Selkirk Auctioneers

A press pin from the 1969 New York "Miracle" Mets, who stunned the baseball world by winning 100 regular-season games, dumping the veteran Atlanta Braves in the first League Championship Series and then crushing a vaunted 1969 Orioles ball club in the World Series, **$275**.

Geppi's Memorabilia Road Show

If only the Red Sox had this many pennants. The work of one Fenway fanatic is compiled into a single auction lot, **$215**.

Heritage Auctions

Lot of five 1960s MLB vintage full-size felt pennants, includes a Kansas City Athletics green felt pennant with yellow piping, tassels and lettering, features player in front of the A at bat inside the stadium; San Francisco Giants blue felt pennant with yellow piping and tassels, white lettering, features Giant in full baseball uniform standing on the Golden Gate Bridge; San Diego Padres red felt pennant with yellow piping and tassels, white lettering, features Padres player at bat in circle and MLB logo in upper left corner, dated 1969; Cincinnati Redlegs red felt pennant with yellow piping, white lettering and logo, features a baseball player with ball head riding a baseball bat over the stadium; and Washington Senators red felt pennant with white tassels, lettering and logo, features player throwing a ball in front of the Capital Building; also includes a 6th pennant that is a later issue: a Detroit Tigers full-size orange felt pennant with brown piping and lettering, features Tiger over Tiger stadium logo and MLB logo in lower left corner, **$130**.

Fusco Auctions

Lot of six 1970s MLB pennants: Mariners, Expos, Cardinals, Padres, Cubs, Reds, approximately 30" each, **$20**.

Hassinger & Courtney Auctioneering

Boston Braves pennant, 28", **$50**.

Hassinger & Courtney Auctioneering

Original New York Giants pennant 26", **$60**.

Saco River Auction

Original full-sized felt pennant from the 1950's Boston Red Sox, multi-color graphic of a baseball player at bat with Fenway Park in the background, hard-to-find maroon felt, **$50**.

Saco River Auction

Vintage Detroit Tigers baseball team pennant, circa 1940s-'50s,
28" x 11-1/2", **$10**.

Cordier Auctions & Appraisals

Rare 1960s California Angels full-size red felt pennant, extremely
difficult to find with this particular logo, showcases an Angel logo in
full baseball uniform on a cracked baseball, yellow piping and tassels,
white lettering, **$50**.

Fusco Auctions

Rare vintage Philadelphia Phillies pennant featuring the Blue Jay
mascot. The Blue Jay mascot was put into use circa 1940s, when
it was applied to the sleeves of the uniforms, as well as pennants
and other memorabilia. It was a result of a nickname contest the
Phillies held in which fans could submit their ideas for a second
team nickname and Blue Jays was the winning choice. However,
the team was still known as the Philadelphia Phillies officially,
28-1/2" x 11", **$30**.

Cordier Auctions & Appraisals

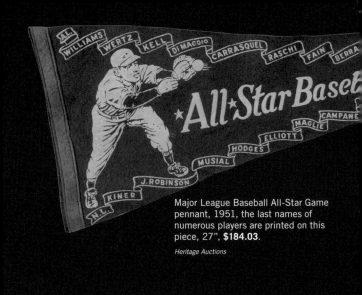

Major League Baseball All-Star Game pennant, 1951, the last names of numerous players are printed on this piece, 27", **$184.03**.

Heritage Auctions

New York Yankees picture pennant, 1961. The 1961 World Series champs were a historically significant team for more than the Fall Classic triumph they enjoyed over the Cincinnati Reds that year. Enthusiasts will remember the epic home run race between Bronx Bomber teammates Mickey Mantle and Roger Maris were embroiled in that year as they chased Babe Ruth's single-season home run mark. The 30" Yankees pennant includes a 5" x 7" team photo embedded within it, **$388.38**.

Heritage Auctions

Chicago Cubs pennant, 1920s, very rare and early style was hoisted by a fan at Wrigley during the days of Gabby Hartnett and Hack Wilson, frame is 35" long, **$507.88**.

Heritage Auctions

Cleveland Indians American League Champions pennant, 1920, which was a season of tragedy and joy. In mid-August, shortstop Ray Chapman was struck by a Carl Mays fastball to the skull and never regained consciousness, and was dead at age twenty-nine. But six weeks later, still wearing black armbands at their left sleeves in memory of their fallen comrade, the Tribe would vanquish the Brooklyn Dodgers to claim the franchise's first ever World Championship. This is a phenomenally scarce felt pennant sold at League Park during the first World Series in Cleveland, with a detailed Native American at left, 20" long, **$2,031.30**.

Heritage Auctions

Two St. Louis Cardinals pennants, **$120**.

Bunte Auction Services, Inc.

A string of San Diego Padres and All-Star Game pennants, **$110**.

Jeff Figler

Four bronze medals with baseball player in a hitting stance, initials PSA in upper right hand corner, screw backs, 1" high, **$10**.

Blueberry Hill Galleries

Sweet Caporal Ty Cobb baseball pin, excellent condition, **$175**.

Dan Morphy Auctions LLC

World Series press pin (New York Yankees) with original design artwork, 1937, 3" x 4.5", **$836.50**.

Heritage Auctions

World Series (Brooklyn Dodgers) press pin, 1916. Diminutive in size but enormous in collecting appeal, the pin allowed one lucky journalist entry to Ebbets Field to watch Games Three and Four of the Dodgers' Fall Classic meeting with Babe Ruth's Boston Red Sox, diameter .75", **$2,868**.

Heritage Auctions

Lot of 10 baseball player pins including a Ted Williams stadium pin, A W&H Never Forgotten Babe Ruth pin, another small Ted Williams pin, three Hall of Fame pins, Ruth, two Gehrigs, and others, some have pitting on back, overall good condition, **$40**.

JMW Auction Service

Joe DiMaggio and Lou Gehrig for New York Yankees, Ted Williams for Boston Red Sox. DiMaggio has light rust and oxidation on back, Gehrig has oxidation on back and Williams is stating to show oxidation, **$600**.

Omaha Auction Center

Sweet Caporal Tris Speaker pin,
Very Good condition, **$60**.

Dan Morphy Auctions LLC.

Baseball club membership pin
back, Very Fine to Near Mint,
15/16" diameter, **$75**.

Dan Morphy Auctions LLC

Vintage Brooklyn Dodgers Jackie Robinson and Roy Campanella
pinbacks, available at Ebbetts Field after the barrier-breaking
Robinson and Roy were changing the hearts of the Brooklyn faithful
as well as the world with their play for the Dodgers. This pair of
1950s pinbacks measures 1-3/4" diameter, **$173.20**.

Heritage Auctions

Cincinnati Reds 1939 pin
with ball and glove, 1939,
excellent condition, **$15**.

Hassinger & Courtney Auctioneering

Baltimore Orioles 1966 World
Champions pin with ribbons and
bat, **$40**.

Hassinger & Courtney Auctioneering

Group of baseball pins including three World Series and one All Star Game, group of two *Sports Illustrated* pins from the 1988 and 1989 World Series, one Balfour Mets World Series pin and one 1991 Toronto All Star Game pin by Peter David, Inc. Pins are in excellent condition, **$50**.

Geppi's Memorabilia Road Show

Four Boston Red Sox pins, made by The Keezer Mfg. Co., Inc., circa 1950s, **$80.**

Bunte Auction Services, Inc.

A 1951 Boston Red Sox Golden Anniversary pin, scarce 10k gold-filled pin was created to commemorate the 50th anniversary of the Boston Red Sox franchise, one of the eight charter teams to form the American League in 1901. The face features an eagle perched atop a blue enamel ring reading "Golden Anniversary." The words "Red Sox 1951" appear in raised lettering on the center, crafted in the shape of a baseball, a faux diamond is inset at top, NRMT condition, 3/4" diameter, **$507.88.**

Heritage Auctions

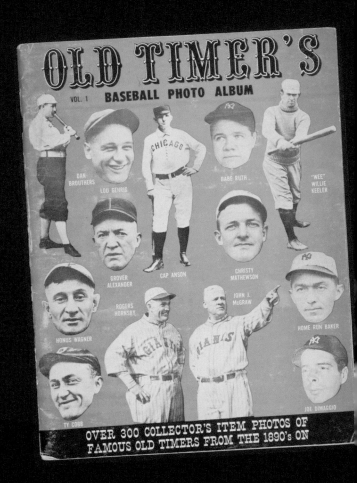

Old Timer's magazine signed by an array of legendary players including Harry Hooper, Rube Marquard, Stanley Coveleski, Waite Hoyt, Ossie Bluege, Joe McCarthy, Leo Durocher, Lefty Grove, Lloyd Waner, Joe Cronin, Bill Dickey, Joe Medwick, Bob Feller, Pete Gray, Ralph Kiner and Joe Garagiola, **$286.80**.

Heritage Auctions

CHAPTER 9

Programs and Other Printed Materials

Game programs have always been popular among collectors. It's not hard to understand why: they're free. And it will come as no surprise to learn that World Series programs are among the most highly cherished of all. They've been produced for the Fall Classic every year since 1903, with two exceptions: 1904 and 1994, when the World Series wasn't played.

The 1903 programs are the "Holy Grail" of World Series programs and can fetch daunting sums, from $50,000 to $100,000, depending on condition.

A 1924 World Series program between the Giants and Senators, autographed by Walter Johnson, went for about $3,000 at auction.

In general, Yankees and Dodgers programs tend to sell for the most money. Programs from 1950 to the present day generally sell for no more than $300.

Program from the 1992 All-Star Game, **$60.**

Jeff Figler

MEDIA GUIDES AND MAGAZINES

Media guides usually contain biographical and statistical information about a team's manager, coaches, and players. They came into use in the 1950s and '60s. And you'll be happy to hear that they're usually affordable and easy to acquire. (And they're a lot lighter than stadium seats.)

Guides before 1940 are usually the most expensive of these

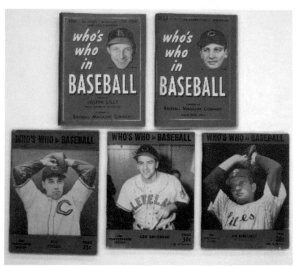

Lot of five assorted 1940s and 1950s *Who's Who In Baseball* magazines, includes: 1941, 1949, 1951, 1952 and 1954, **$20**.

B.S. Slosberg, Inc. Auctioneers

collectibles, as are the guides from the first year of a team's existence. Cases in point: The 1961 Los Angeles Angels guide goes for about $250, and a 1962 New York Mets media guide will run you around $650. Current year guides can be had for about $15 to $20.

In addition to press guides, other printed material commands respect as well. Most issues of *The Sporting News* from the 1960s and '70s range from $20-$50, while the issues documenting such memorable events as Roger Maris' chase of Babe Ruth's home run record in 1961 sells for upwards of $150. Issues featuring iconic figures can fetch up to $100. That's also true for issues from 1974, when Hank Aaron was chasing the Babe's career home run mark. Alas, old newspapers and magazines have minimal value, except to a local fan base.

Issues of *Sports Illustrated* are highly collectible. The magazine started publishing in August 1954, with Milwaukee Braves star Eddie Mathews on the cover. To attract readers, *SI* included a three-page foldout of 1954 Topps baseball cards. That first issue, dated August 16, 1954, is worth keeping: it's now worth about $200, if it's in excellent condition. The second issue, dated August 23, 1954, interestingly enough, can be worth even more. Why? People make a point of keeping an inaugural

Pair of 1970s Baseball Championship Series milestone ticket stubs, includes 1972 Championship Series National West vs National East Game 4 Ticket at Riverfront Stadium; this is the game ticket commemorates Roberto Clemente's last home run; also includes September 12, 1979 Rain Check stub for the Boston Red Sox game at Fenway Park; this ticket commemorates Carl Yastrzemski's 3,000th hit, **$40**.

Fusco Auctions

effort, but often overlook the second issue of a magazine. Autographed copies of *SI* increase the value.

TICKETS

Pickers should note that full tickets, as well as ticket stubs, are relatively new collectibles. They're especially appealing to collectors looking to amass as much of an individual player's memorabilia as possible. Most times a collector taking this approach is looking to acquire tickets from games that were significant for a slugger. For example, they'll want a full ticket or stub from the game in which the player collected his 200th career home run, or they'll be on the prowl for a ticket from the day a pitcher won his 100th career game.

Other times, collectors have been railroaded. Case in point: At one antiques sale, a person forked over $60 for what he thought were two 19th century railroad tickets. He did not get what he paid for—and he didn't mind. Neither would you, because one of those tickets turned out to be to a baseball game from the late 1860s or '70s, and the other was to a baseball players' convention in 1867. Experts say they could be the earliest tickets in baseball history and are worth several hundred dollars apiece. Not bad for a $60 investment.

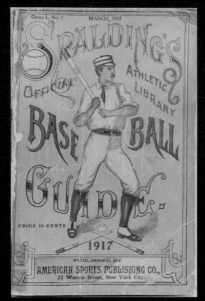

A 1917 *Spalding Baseball Guide*, **$150**.

Saco River Auction

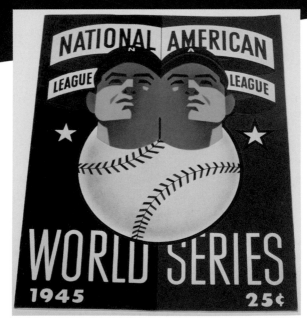

A 1945 *World Series* program, Chicago Cubs versus Detroit Tigers, **$150**.

Bunte Auction Services, Inc.

Extremely rare 1972 *Kodak World Baseball Classic* program (aka World Baseball Championship) in excellent condition; scorecard unmarked. The round-robin tournament was between the champions of the American Association, International League, Pacific Coast League, the Hawaii Islanders and a group of All-Star players from Latin America Winter Leagues. The program was sent to one of the National Association general managers, along with a letter of intent included in this lot, **$25**.

Fusco Auctions

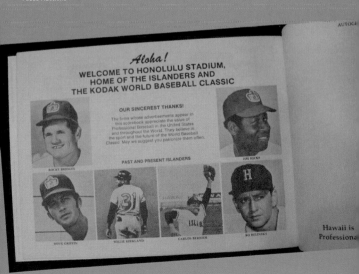

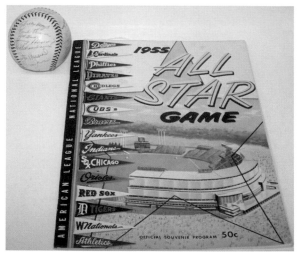

A *1955 All Star Game* program and ball, game played in Milwaukee, ball signed by National League team including Hank Aaron, Stan Musial, Stan Lopata, Eddie Mathews, Del Crandall, Ernie Banks, Luis Arroyo, Don Newcombe, Duke Snider, Joe Nuxhall, Ted Kluszewski, Robin Roberts, Randy Jackson, Red Schoendienst, Harry Haddix, Frank Thomas, Willie Mays, Johnny Logan, Gene Conley, Del Ennis, Smoky Burgess, Sam Jones, Gene Baker, manager Leo Durocher, coach Mayo Smith, Milwaukee coach Bob Keeley, Milwaukee pitchers Chet Nichols and Bob Buhl, program has fill-in box scores, including extra innings, **$550**.

Bunte Auction Services, Inc.

The 1958 *All Star Game* program, featured Casey Stengel as the American League manager and players such as Mickey Mantle, Luis Aparicio, Stan Musial, Ernie Banks, Willie Mays and Henry Aaron as starters; other players were Ted Williams, Yogi Berra, Whitey Ford, Warren Spahn, Bob Purkey, etc. Program also lists Hall of Fame candidates Williams and Musial, also some great old advertisements, condition is very good to excellent, **$70**.

Affiliated Auctions

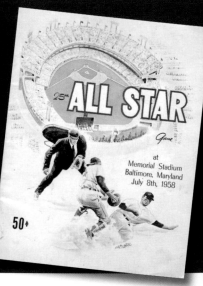

A 2003 official *World Series* program with six signatures from team members with certificate, 10" x 8-1/4", **$30**.

International Auction Gallery

A 1933 *Official Score Book* and signed ball of the first All-Star Game, **$7,500**.

Jeff Figler

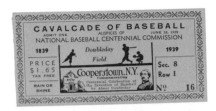

A 1939 Baseball Hall of Fame grand opening program and ticket stub. The Centennial season of baseball is remembered for the debut of Ted Williams and the tragic departure of Lou Gehrig, but it could be argued that the most significant event of the season took place in a sleepy little upstate New York village called Cooperstown. Here are one lucky baseball fan's personal mementoes from the grand opening of the Baseball Hall of Fame, an event that saw the official immortalization of Ruth, Cobb, Wagner and several other Dead Ball and Golden Age legends. The program from the day's events contains scorecards for the Collins vs. Wagners contest at center (unscored), **$896.25**.

Heritage Auctions

A program from the 1998 World Series, **$55**.

Jeff Figler

Sports Illustrated magazine featuring "Casey at the Bat," **$20**.

Jeff Figler

Two ticket stubs from Stan Musial's last game on September 27, 1963, **$280**.

Jeff Figler

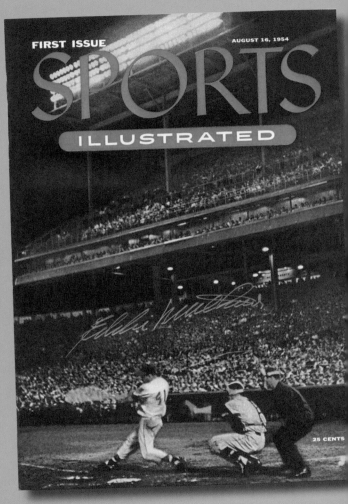

Sports Illustrated first issue, August 16, 1954, signed by Eddie
Matthews PSADNA Authenticated, this first issue also includes a
special bound-in supplement of 27 Topps baseball card reproductions
featuring players such as Ted Williams, Jackie Robinson, Willie Mays,
and Duke Snider, unsigned edition sells for $299; this one sold at
auction for **$334.60**.

Heritage Auctions

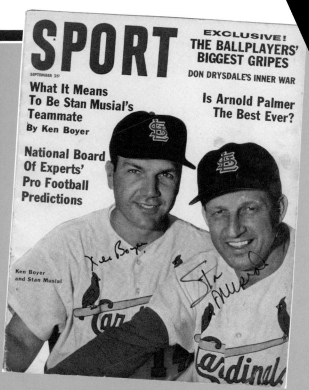

Stan Musial and Ken Boyer signed September 1962 issue of *Sport* magazine, signatures in blue Sharpie are clear, clean, and bold, **$286.80**.

Heritage Auctions

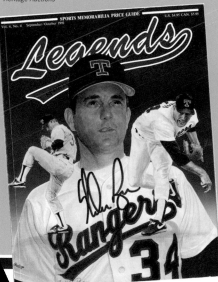

Nolan Ryan signed *Legends* magazine, the Texas legend has signed the cover in bold blue Sharpie. Ryan's record 7 no hitters, and 5,714 strikeouts will most likely never be approached, **$51**.

Heritage Auctions

Lot of three publications with Mickey Mantle on the cover: includes two vintage *Sport Magazines* and a newer comic, all in Good/VG condition; includes 1959 *Dell Sports Magazine* "Who's Who in the Big Leagues," July-Sept Vol. I, No 9 issue; shows a young Mantle on the cover with a story inside; also includes April 1963 *Baseball Magazine* featuring Mays and Mantle on the cover as "Baseball's Most Exciting Players"; and also includes December 1991 Magnum Comics Mickey Mantle Vol. I, No. 1 (Baseball's Greatest Heroes) issue in mint condition, **$30**.

Fusco Auctions

Extremely rare 1870 Philadelphia Athletics Baseball Club Season ticket with punched game numbers of games attended. Very unusual early season ticket dated 1870. The ticket is earlier than any other one housed in the Baseball Hall of Fame, **$4,750**.

Saco River Auction

A 2004 World Series Game 4 full ticket and 2006 Curt Schilling 3,000 Strikeout full ticket, also included is an unsigned Schilling 8" x 10" photo, **$137.43**.

Heritage Auctions

Lot of early baseball game tickets, 1911, **$70**.

The Cobbs Auctioneers, LLC.

Extremely rare 1867 National Association of Baseball Players Eleventh Annual Convention ticket dated December 11th 1867 at 11AM, this is the first such ticket known to exist, **$6,250**.

...aco River Auction

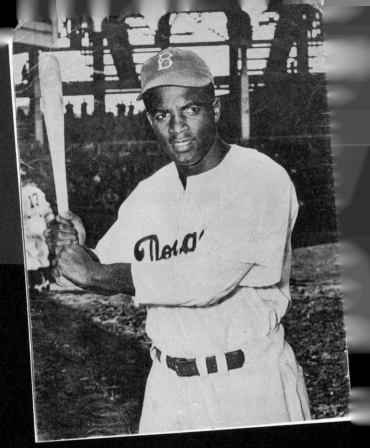

A 1950s Jackie Robinson signed magazine photograph. The pioneering Hall of Famer signed in 6/10 blue ink, "Best wishes, Jackie Robinson," 8" x 10", **$448.13**.

Heritage Auctions

CHAPTER 10

Photos, Paintings, and Posters

Baseball photographs, including wire service photos, can be stunning collectibles. Vintage photos of star players have sold for thousands of dollars, especially if they're signed.

Old postcards with baseball backgrounds, or with the players themselves on the front, are big "hits" as well, with some collectors. Stadium postcards are particularly popular. Postcards can be purchased easily, and are affordable, so if you're drawn to them, I strongly encourage you to take that route.

MOVIE POSTERS

With "movie posters" staring you dead in the eye, you might be wondering if you've just walked into a book about an entirely different kind of collectible, but no, I'm talking about those great baseball movies in which fact and fiction were put into Hollywood's magical blender.

Baseball has a long history of providing big box office returns for Tinseltown. However, let's begin our review, if you will, with more recently released films. They include *Moneyball* with Brad Pitt, Jonah Hill, and Philip Seymour Hoffman; *Bang the Drum Slowly* starring Michael Moriarty, a young Robert De Niro, and Vincent Gardenia; *Bull Durham*, with Kevin Costner, Susan Sarandon, and Tim Robbins; *Field of Dreams* with Costner again, along with his buds James Earl Jones and Ray Liotta; and *The Natural*, one of Robert Redford's finest films, with terrific performances by Robert Duvall and Glenn Close.

With all that star power, you might think a full-size movie

ster, usually 27 inches by 41 inches, would cost a bundle. Not at all. You can pick them up for about $20.

But there's one film poster that will cost you many times that amount. It's the 1927 *Babe Comes Home*, based on the short story, "Said with Soap," by Gerald Beaumont. The Babe in the film is none other than Babe Ruth. He plays the fictional Babe Dugan in the film, which tells the story of a home run hitter for the Los Angeles Angels who has a habit of chewing tobacco while he's playing. Thus, his uniforms need to be cleaned by Snow White Laundry.

Vernie is the worker who lands the cleaning assignment. After numerous scrubbings, she goes to a baseball game, and Dugan promptly hits a ball right in her eye. Of course she's pretty. Of course he apologizes. And, of course, romance blossoms even as her eye blackens and his uniform whitens.

But the tobacco remains a habit, even as Vernie tries valiantly to dissuade him from using it. But he's a charmer, as Ruth reputedly was in real life, and Vernie finally relents, and actually, gives him some tobacco herself.

He hits a grand slam with her in attendance, and afterward decides never to use tobacco again, realizing that it was his love for Vernie, not tobacco, that helped him.

Okay, so the script didn't win the Oscar, but one of the posters for *Babe Comes Home* won the collectibles equivalent of the golden statue: it sold for $138,000. Even lobby cards of that film sell from $3,000 to $12,000.

Typically, movie costumes from baseball epics don't cost as much. However, a jacket worn by Frank Sinatra in the 1949 musical, *Take Me Out to the Ball Game*, went for $6,000 at auction. A uniform worn by Madonna in the 1992 movie, *A League of Their Own*, fetched almost $4,000. But a Detroit Tigers replica jersey worn by Tommy Lee Jones in the movie, *Cobb*, sold for slightly more than $400, or about 10 percent of Madonna's threads.

A 1927 *Babe Comes Home* one-sheet movie poster, one of just two examples known. Sports-related posters have enjoyed popular demand for many years, and none more so than those that actually feature real sports legends. This one sheet depicts the greatest legend to ever play the game of baseball, the Sultan of Swat, Babe Ruth. During his career, Ruth was the game's elite slugger, and his fame led producers to feature him in several films. Some of those films, such as this one and *Headin' Home* from 1920, cast him as the lead, while other films found him in cameos as in Harold Lloyd's *Speedy* in 1928 and *The Pride of the Yankees* in 1942. Due to the fragile nature of vintage posters, this example has been mounted on linen, 27" x 41", **$83,650**.

Heritage Auctions

Shane Victorino signed photograph, 8" x 10", COA by Major League Baseball, **$10**.

Stephenson's Auction

A photo of the 1958 St. Louis Cardinals, **$20**.

Jeff Figler

A signed photo of Pete Gray, the one-armed St. Louis Browns player, 1945, **$75**.

Jeff Figler

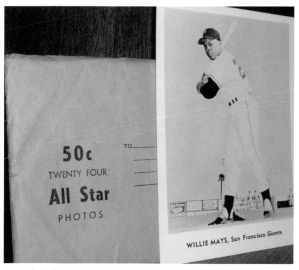

Pack of All-Star photos, 1962, including Willie Mays, **$35**.

Jeff Figler

Early cabinet photo, albumen print on card stock with blank back, depicting three players in dress uniforms, two with bats, no identification or photographer's stamp, fourth quarter 19th century, 6-1/2" x 4-1/4", **$120**.

Jeffrey S. Evans & Associates

Framed and matted homage to Fred Hutchinson, a Major League pitcher for the Detroit Tigers and a manager for three Major League teams, includes his baseball card, a vintage photograph and his autograph on a slip of paper, framed measurement 21" x 17", **$40**.

Klein James

Baseball legends Babe Ruth and Lou Gehrig circa 1920s, posing on their wood weapons. This "International Newsreel" photo measures at 8" x 10", **$1,135.25**.

Heritage Auctions

Hall of Famer Larry Doby signed photograph,
signed in 10/10 blue Sharpie, 8" x 10", **$40**.

Heritage Auctions

Al Kaline signed photograph, graded a Gem Mint PSA 10,
signed in blue Sharpie, 8" x 10", **$50**.

Heritage Auctions

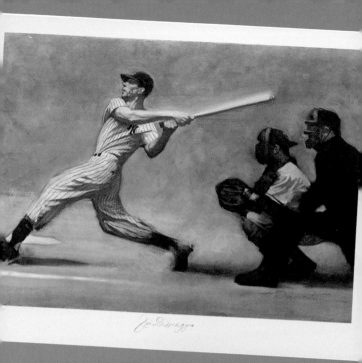

This masterful 1974 Joe DiMaggio painting by Harvey Dinnerstein was utilized for famous *Sports Illustrated* "Living Legends" lithographs. Titled "The Wide Swing," it's the most recognizable DiMaggio artwork in existence and the oil portrait captures a legend at the peak of his abilities an unbroken chain of fifty-six games with a recorded base hit, the artist's signature appears at lower right of the 24" x 32" canvas, **$89,625**.

Heritage Auctions

An original LeRoy Neiman painting of Yankee Star Phil Rizzuto, **$75,000**.

Jeff Figler

An original artwork featuring Phillies home run legend Michael Jack Schmidt, signed in Mint blue Sharpie by the great Hall of Famer, presented on an illustration board, 22" x 28", **$119.50**.

Heritage Auctions

Bull Durham (Orion, 1988), one sheet poster, unrestored with bright color and a clean overall appearance, folded, Very Fine-, 27" x 41", **$23**.

Heritage Auctions

Field of Dreams (Universal, 1989), one sheet poster, unrestored with bright color and a clean overall appearance, Very Fine, 27" x 40", **$20**.

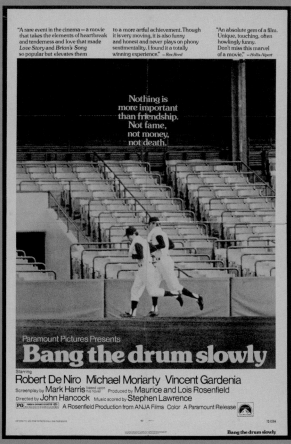

Bang the Drum Slowly (Paramount, 1973), one sheet poster, unrestored with bright color and a clean overall appearance, Very Fine, 27" x 41", **$25**.

Heritage Auctions

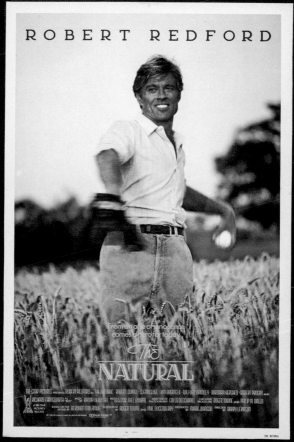

The Natural (Tri-Star, 1984), one sheet poster, unrestored, Fine/Very Fine, 27" x 41", **$26**.

Heritage Auctions

Without a doubt, this is the finest baseball machine ever produced by any company and is a must have for a collector of arcade machines, as well as those who are baseball collectors. Featured are the infamous baseball players of the 1937 World Series games: DiMaggio, Gehrig, Dickey, Chapman, etc. at bat and in the outfield Medwick, Dykes, Dean, Averill, etc. After a coin is deposited, a ball appears from the umpire's chest and is handed off to the pitcher, who then throws the ball to you in one of a variety of pitches, and you swing your bat. The accurate system of balls and strikes is kept by means of steel balls in marked troughs. Many options can occur: hitting directly to the shortstop for an out, down the 1st or 3rd base line for a home run, a foul ball, double, or a direct shot to Dizzy Dean, the pitcher, for an out. All the while, the three outfielders and four infielders are nervously twitching and moving slightly from left to right, positioning themselves and awaiting your mastery at bat. The game is 40" w x 54" h x 29-1/2" d and sold at auction for **$33,350**.

James D. Julia, Inc.

CHAPTER 11

Board and Other Baseball Games

Baseball board games starring Babe Ruth have been popular over many decades, but even having the Sultan of Swat in your lineup ultimately couldn't help a board game nudge out the Ethan Allen All-Star Baseball game in the popularity sweepstakes. But first, let's clear up some confusion about the name of this collectible.

The All-Star Baseball board game was introduced by Candace-Ellis, a Chicago firm, in 1941. However, the name of the game was changed to Ethan Allen All-Star Baseball several years later to honor the inventor, Ethan Allen.

Parker Brothers "Peg Baseball" game with original contents, circa 1908, **$125**.

Copake Auction, Inc.

Allen was a solid big leaguer for thirteen years in the 1920s and 1930s. He later worked for the National League before coaching the Yale University baseball team from 1946 to 1968. His most famous team member? None other than President George H. Bush.

In the Ethan Allen All-Star Baseball board game that I played, current players were pitted against all-stars from the past. Discs of each player, portraying accurate statistics, were spun. And the better team on any particular day won. It all de-ended on where the needle of the spinner landed on the disc.

Although the game was originally designed for boys nine to twelve years of age, it truly has been enjoyed by "children of all ages." In fact, it ranks as one of the most important board games of all time. It was first sold in 1941, and then re-issued annually until 1993. A hiatus ensued until the game was revived in 2004.

While the game has changed through the years—and the discs and spinners have been altered from their original design—the game's basic concept has remained the same.

Older editions of Ethan Allen All-Star Baseball have sold for a few hundred dollars, depending on condition.

Strat-O-Matic Baseball, first produced in 1961, has been a steady competitor of the Ethan Allen All-Star game. Strat-O-Matic has survived handily, and today can be played online. Strat-O-Matic remains strongly innovative, and recently started marketing a Negro League stars version as well.

Baseball card dispensing machine of Exhibit Baseball Cards, **$80**.

Jeff Figler

5 Cent "All American Baseball Game" floor model, mechanical, Manikin Playfield Players Skill Game circa 1929-1931, by Amusement Machine Corp., **$55,000**.

Victorian Casino Antiques

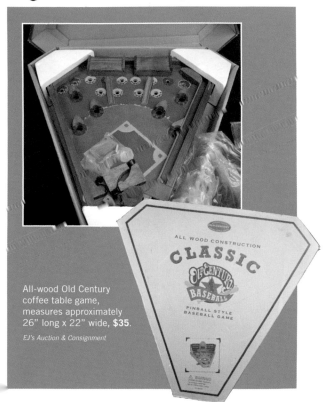

All-wood Old Century coffee table game, measures approximately 26" long x 22" wide, **$35**.

EJ's Auction & Consignment

US Savings Bonds Pegged baseball game, **$30**.

Saco River Auction

Lawson's Patent Baseball Playing Cards, Lawson Card Co., Boston, MA, 1884, 36 (complete) cards, three value cards, two rule pamphlets, OB, EX, earliest known baseball card game, **$300**.

Potter & Potter Auctions

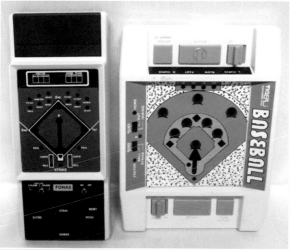

Two computer baseball games including *Two-Player Baseball* and *Tiger Computer Baseball*, with original boxes, **$10**.

Specialists of the South, Inc.

Recreation of 1 Cent 1931 Pace MFG. Baseball Flipball Skill Game countertop trade stimulator with key, **$300**.

Victorian Casino Antiques

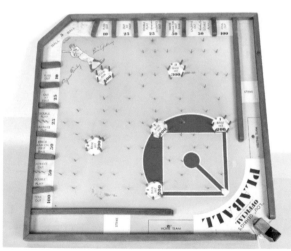

Circa 1940 baseball game, paper litho on board with metal pins, no marbles, 18" square with an image of the legendary Lou Gehrig at the top, **$110**.

NETTE Auctions

Complete Quaker Oals baseball game with instructions card, dated 1934, game is titled "Ask Me, The Game of Baseball Facts," with advertising for Quaker Puffed Rice, copyright Quaker Oats Co. and printed by Einson Freeman Co. Inc., 27 pieces, **$75**.

Fontaines Auction Gallery

Mickey Mantle board game, 1957, signed by the Yankees legend, with its original box, **$250.95**.

Heritage Auctions

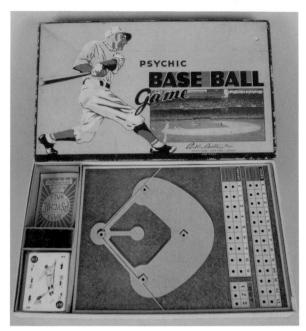

Game made by Parker Brothers with original box, great graphics of an early baseball game on the box, Very Good condition, 16-1/2" long, **$50**.

Dan Morphy Auctions LLC

Baseball Penny Drop Trade Stimulator Game, pine wood case has a silvered coin slot in the top and frame around the glass, drop the penny onto the vertical game board with pins directing the penny to various end slots in the bottom, decal on the game board reads "Play Baseball," with point scoring indicator decals, has back board with lock and key, numbered 161, refinished, 15" high x 10" wide x 6-3/4" deep, **$250**.

Fontaines Auction Gallery

Northwestern Products Poosh-M-Up 5 Game Streamliner Pinball-Style Game with instructions, five games: Twenty-One, Put-N-Take, Baseball, Bagatelle, and Pennants, **$50**.

Victorian Casino Antiques

Early baseball game, circa 1930, manufactured by All Fair Toys and Games, a pitcher would project a ball on the surface to the batter whose spring-wound bat would strike the ball, sending it hopefully into the outfield for a hit, a hole at top for a home run, or into a fielder's depression in the tin surface for an out. Regrettably, the fixtures are lost, including bat, "players," and balls, but mechanism remains operable, instructions are pasted to underside, 18" x 24-1/2" wood frame with painted tin surface, **$80**.

Alexander Historical Auctions LLC

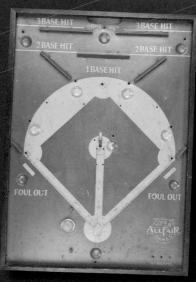

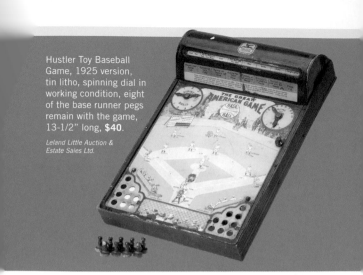

Hustler Toy Baseball Game, 1925 version, tin litho, spinning dial in working condition, eight of the base runner pegs remain with the game, 13-1/2" long, **$40**.

Leland Little Auction & Estate Sales Ltd.

Central Manufacturing Co. Hi Fly Baseball Countertop Trade Stimulator Game, 5 Cent coin skill game with coin slot on the right side and flip lever in the front, the coin flips into the playing field and bounces through the pegged game board coming to a rest at one of the game situation, circa 1946, in good working original condition, 22" high x 16-1/2" wide x 11-1/2" deep, **$750**.

Fontaines Auction Gallery

Circa 1890 Bliss wooden carnival game, screams Victorian-era baseball, from the striped uniform to the lettered belt, to the tall laced boots to the crazy mustache. The little gentleman stands 22" high, with four cloth pockets to receive tossed baseballs. Wood construction, with a swiveling base for standing and storage, included is a photocopy of a period catalog page listing these at ten dollars per dozen; only example known, **$4,418.25**.

Heritage Auctions

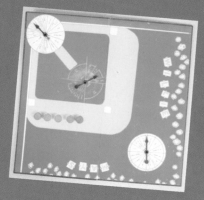

Willie Mays' Baseball Game, made by Oliver Game Company, marked 1954 on box, cover also says 1954 Most Valuable Player, includes game board with some wear, especially underneath spinners, no game pieces, Very Good condition, box is 14" long, **$275**.

Dan Morphy Auctions LLC

Unusual Pro Baseball bame, complete in original box, 1946, **$110**.

Carden Family Auction Service

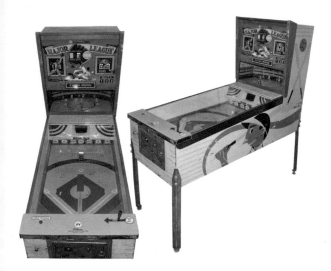

Working coin-operated machine has movable base runners and backdrop, plastic home run panel has some wear damage from use, some wear to case, 65" long x 72" high x 24-1/2" deep, **$600**. The front graphics of the game are shown in a close-up below.

Mosby & Co. Auctions

Vintage Baseball
Poosh M Up
Game, no case,
13" x 20", **$14**.

Pioneer Auction Gallery

Game of Ship's Baseball, full boxed example of this rare baseball
board game dates from 1912, a game board is included that has the
same image shown on the box cover, which also contains colored
playing tokens, playing cards and the games rules, **$191.20**.

Heritage Auctions

Vintage Play "Bambino" litho, tin and wood base, circa 1930s, table baseball skill game, with accessories, Pat. Pending Johnson Store Equipment Company, Elgin, Illinois, **$100**.

Victorian Casino Antiques

1 Cent Marvel's Pop-Up Baseball Countertop Skill Game, circa 1936, wood and glass cabinet, all original, works with keys, **$475**.

Victorian Casino Antiques

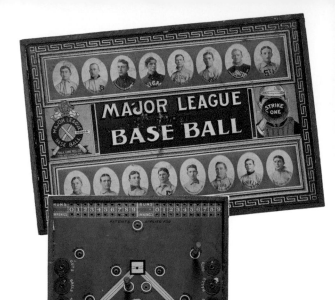

Major League Indoor Baseball Game, 1913, that's the famous multi-million dollar Honus Wagner T206 image third from left on the bottom row. Every top Hall of Famer is here: Baker, Cobb, Lajoie, Walsh, Speaker, Chase, Johnson, Wallace, Mathewson, Chance, Bresnahan, with brightly colored artwork surrounding upon the hinged wooden lid. Game cards are not present, **$1,912.**

Heritage Auctions

Official Baseball Card Game, 1970, complete children's game from Milton Bradley includes all playing cards and game board, **$27**.

Heritage Auctions

Zimmer's Baseball game, extraordinary portraiture of 19th century legends including Buck Ewing, Cy Young and "Sliding Billy" Hamilton, eighteen Major League players adorn the playing surface, a roster packed with names that today appear in Cooperstown bronze. In the field we find Buck Ewing (catcher), Amos Rusie (pitcher), Dan Brouthers (first base), John Montgomery Ward (second base), John Glasscock (shortstop), George Davis (third base),Sam Thompson (right field), Jimmy McAleer (center field) and Billy Hamilton (left field). Portraits in the dugout: Cy Young, Kid Nichols, W. Zimmer (unknown, perhaps related to the game maker), Jacob Virtue, Bid McPhee, George Davies, Patsy Tebeau, Ed Delehanty and Germany Smith. Pictured in front of the plate is accomplished Native American catcher "Chief" Zimmer, **$29,875**.

Heritage Auctions

This 1923 New York Yankees World Championship pocket watch presented to Babe Ruth is considered one of the most significant articles of New York Yankees memorabilia that exists. The pentagonal 14-karat gold timepiece was part of a set given to Ruth and his Yankees teammates after they beat their rivals, the New York Giants, in the 1923 World Series. Ruth batted .368 and hit three home runs in the series, the first of the Yankees' 27 world championships. The watch is engraved with a picture of a pitcher, hitter and catcher and a ball in flight and inscribed, "Presented by Baseball Commissioner to George H. Ruth." It sold at auction in 2014 for **$717,000**.

Heritage Auctions

CHAPTER 12

Jewelry

Jewelry is a broad category, and I use it only for accuracy's sake. In truth, for the most part, collectors interested in player jewelry never shift their focus from an athlete's fingers, where his championship ring generally perches.

Championship team personnel—players, coaches, and front office workers—are given rings, while support staff are bequeathed replica rings.

The value of the ring often depends on who wore it, so the cost can range from a few thousand dollars on up.

Now, it could save you money

Brooklyn Dodgers ring, 1930s, stadium item, **$125**.

Dan Morphy Auctions, LLC

to keep in mind that players almost always keep their rings, so what you're going to be offered for sale in most cases will be a salesman's sample ring. Doesn't have quite the cachet, does it?

Rings are generally auctioned or sold at trade shows. They're plenty popular, and for good reason: they're an excellent way to remember a team's championship year.

A 500 Home Run Club ring in 14k gold, set with individually cut
diamonds inset within a crown, flanking one side of the ring are
names from the American League: Williams, Mantle, Robinson, Babe
Ruth, etc.; the other side has names from the National League:
Aaron, Mays, Mathews, etc. The inside of the ring is marked 17 of 20,
and LGB 14k. Ring size 12. Overall weight 40.9 grams, **$1,050**.

Klein James

Cleveland Indians MLB men's size 11 ring, featuring Cleveland
Indians in gold lettering with Chief Wahoo in the center, sides have
the MLB logo and read Major League Baseball, **$40**.

Fusco Auctions

World Series
Championship ring,
Cardinals, 1946,
belonged to Theodore
"Cork" Wilks, the
Cardinals' pitcher at the
time, 14k gold center
diamond of approximately
a half carat, set in red,
the mount reads, "St.
Louis Cardinals World
Champions," the side
shanks of the ring
feature the Cardinals'
"Redbird" logo with
"1946" inscribed below,
inner is stamped 14k and
engraved, "Presented
to Theodore Wilks from,
Baseball Commissioner,"
$4,000.

Manor Auctions

A 1949-60 New York Yankees press pins charm bracelet, recalling a dozen seasons of Yankee greatness, in chronological order, and of World Series format unless otherwise noted, are: 1949, 1950, 1951, 1952, 1953, 1955, 1956, 1957, 1958, 1960 All-Star Game, 1960. Eleven charms/pins in total, ranging from VG to EX-MT, **$956**.

Heritage Auctions

A 1993 Toronto Blue Jays World Championship ring. Attempts to reclaim baseball's throne for the United States failed this year as the Philadelphia Phillies fell in six to the Toronto Blue Jays, who repeated as World Champs with a dramatic Joe Carter walk-off blast. Face holds forty-six round brilliant-cut diamonds with a total carat weight of .60, team logo bird and double-Canadian flag imagery appears, with "World Champions 1993" ringing perimeter in raised lettering. left shank reads, "Toronto Blue Jays, 1993 World Series, Back to Back 92-93," right shank provides recipient's surname "Demy" and the symbol of the American League. Interior band is stamped "Tiffany 14k 585" and measures to a size eight. Custom ring box and all Tiffany packaging is present, **$9,560**.

Heritage Auctions

This circa 1948 official Babe Ruth wristwatch is a bit more affordable than his pocket watch. Factory signed and hallmarked with polished chrome top, sides, bezel and lugs, with circular satin sand marked case, **$250**.

Echoes Antiques & Auction Gallery, Inc.

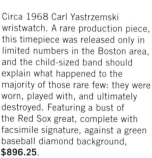

Circa 1968 Carl Yastrzemski wristwatch. A rare production piece, this timepiece was released only in limited numbers in the Boston area, and the child-sized band should explain what happened to the majority of those rare few: they were worn, played with, and ultimately destroyed. Featuring a bust of the Red Sox great, complete with facsimile signature, against a green baseball diamond background, **$896.25**.

Heritage Auctions

CHAPTER 13

How to Value, Flip and Negotiate Memorabilia

If you want to become an experienced baseball picker and sell what you find to collectors and dealers, you have to become knowledgeable about baseball memorabilia and know which types of items sell, how to negotiate, and how to flip items.

FINDING THE VALUE OF YOUR BASEBALL MEMORABILIA

Most of the baseball memorabilia collectors of the world are also passionate about their items. As a general rule, they are meticulous and astute about their collection. They want their collection, let's say, of cards or pennants, or even bobbing head dolls, to be complete, and will always be on the outlook to enhance or reshape their collection. Likewise, they usually stay on top of what their baseball collection might be worth.

How do they go about knowing the value of their items? Well, first let's remember the old maxim that the value of an item is the amount of money that someone is willing to pay for it. Value will depend on condition, scarcity, and desirability (or as some people will say, demand). There are various types of value, including the fair market value (such as through auctions), the wholesale value, the insurance value, the retail value, and even the estate or tax value. But most collectors are not too concerned about which type of value is being analyzed; they just want to have a pretty good idea of what their items are worth.

WAYS YOU CAN LEARN THE WORTH OF ITEMS

- **PRICE GUIDES.** If you collect baseball cards, and let's face it, that has included most of us at one time or another, the two best guides are *The Standard Catalog of Vintage Baseball Cards* by Krause Publications and *The Beckett Almanac of Baseball Cards and Collectibles*. They will give you a great idea of card values based on condition. Both guides are updated regularly.

- **AUCTION RESULTS.** This is another great way to help determine value, especially if you have an item that is the same, or nearly identical, to what was auctioned. However, it is possible that the item that you are comparing with yours was part of a bidding war between two or more bidders, and the high bid was way higher than expected. Does that make the value of your item the same as the high bid? Probably not. The reverse can occur as well, and maybe there was only one bidder who bid the minimum. Does that deflate the value of your item? Probably not. Be careful, also, to look at final auction results, not estimates. There are several auction houses involved with baseball items, including Leland's, Grey Flannel, Heritage, and Robert Edward Auctions.

- **SPORTS COLLECTIBLES DEALERS.** Dealers are excellent resources to help someone determine value. Usually local dealers will be most helpful with such items as cards, programs, bats, photos, baseballs, and even pennants. Most local dealers will not display high-end items such as game-used material; that is usually the role of auction houses. But if you are a casual picker or collector, primarily of baseball cards, a local dealer can give you a good idea of what your cards are worth. Remember to ask the dealer to tell you what the cards are worth, not what he or she would pay you for them. Of course, the dealer wants to make a profit and run a business. Generally speaking, the wholesale value of an item will be anywhere from a third to a half of what the dealer's retail price will be. It is also possible that the dealer has such a surplus of common cards and other items, he or she may not want to purchase what you have. Of course, if you have a Derek Jeter or a Mickey Mantle card, that might be another story.

- **APPRAISAL SERVICES.** Nowadays, appraisal services are used primarily for grading cards. Ever since Professional Sports Authenticators (PSA) put a slab on the finest Honus Wagner card to date, a number of companies besides PSA have provided similar services, such as Sportscard Guaranty Corporation (SGC), and Beckett Grading Services (BGS). Some appraisal companies will also authenticate items such as jerseys and caps, as well as autographs. Having items graded and appraised will raise the value of the item as well. These companies will charge a fee for their services, but it may indeed be worth the cost.

Many collectors will go to sports shows in their area or even to the annual National Sports Collectors Convention. There you can meet a host of vendors selling their stuff. If you bring your items with you, it is possible you can get several opinions of the value of your memorabilia.

As a picker, you should keep in mind that autographed items are worth more than the same item without a signature. Hopefully, the signature can be easily read, such as Tom Glavine's or Tony Gwynn's. Don't try to read Greg Maddux's signature (See Page 74).

If you have a high-end item such as a jersey or bat of a Hall-of-Famer, it would be to your benefit to know the provenance of the item.

GRADING BASEBALL ITEMS

Pickers are conscious that the condition of an item will greatly determine its value. Just like the marketing mantra, "location, location, location," for pickers their mantra is often "condition, condition, condition." And what baseball items are pickers likely to pick? You got it. Baseball cards. Go to any garage or yard sale and even estate sales. What do you see, sometimes in caches of boxes? Baseball cards. Other items, such as programs, are often lying around as well. And an item's condition will determine its grade.

Although there are no hard and fast rules on grading, and grading is arbitrary and subjective, there has been a movement to try to standardize grading. Pickers will often see that some cards have a slab, which clearly identifies that a card has been graded by a company such as Beckett Grading Services (BGS), Professional Sports Authenticators (PSA), Sportscard Guaranty (SGC), or others.

Some pickers prefer cards that are graded, some do not. Take for example, an Ozzie Smith rookie card from 1978. Assume it was graded Excellent by PSA. A picker will be restricted by the card being Excellent, and cannot then sell it as a Mint. In some instances a picker will benefit from the professional grade, as it is proof of the condition of the card.

Oftentimes, sellers will see a shoebox full of Topps cards, let's say from 1984. Instead of carefully sorting through the stacks to identify any stars, who might command a little bit more money, most sellers will not take the time to do so. Pickers will take the time to examine the cards, and possibly find some treasures.

The generally accepted grades that are most common are Mint, Near Mint, Excellent, Very Good, Good, Fair, and Poor grades. For more information on this grading scale and examples of cards in each grade, see Pages 51-57.

Many pickers have a "wish list" of cards in their wallet. Pickers carry such a list for not only cards, but also for 45s, albums, magazines, even books. Remember the old cliché that one man's rubbish (my word) is another person's treasure. I have known collectors who will be on the outlook for particular items, and sure enough, have found them by using their worn-out "wish list" that they pulled from their wallet. Pickers will carry a "wish list" for others as well when they pick.

As a picker, you should be not only concerned with grading, but also with condition. Look at a card's corners, as well as any trimming, creases, and border issues. Veteran pickers are well aware of the importance of corners. To maximize profits, pickers will look at corners as if on cue. Ideally, the corners will be sharp and crisp. If they are even slightly worn or rounded, red flags appear, and the baseball player on the card better be a superstar.

Stay away from trimmed cards. Naturally, a pair of scissors can help to make the corners sharper, improve the centering, and remove the wear. When a card is trimmed, it is noticeable when it is measured and compared with a normal-sized card. Trimming significantly reduces the value of a card.

Optimally, a card will be centered perfectly from side-to-side and top-to-bottom. Good luck! Of course, on the flip side, if a card was 0/100, that would mean that all of the borders are totally on one side. You certainly don't want that. Consider yourself in the ballpark with a 60/40 or 65/35 ratio.

Finally, seasoned pickers will look for stains, fading, writing, holes, and even rubber band marks. It used to be common practice for kids to put rubber bands around groups of cards. Well, if the bands were not removed for an indefinite amount of time, the top and bottom cards would have an unwelcome mark. Take the case of the 1952 Topps set. The first card of that valuable set is of Brooklyn Dodger Andy Pafko. The lucky picker who finds a Pafko card needs to look for rubber band marks. Another common practice was for kids to put cards on their bicycle spokes so that a noise would be heard when you pedaled. Can you imagine ruining a 1952 Topps Mickey Mantle number 311 card because it was used to create noise? There's a reason for that old expression, "Boys will be boys."

But keep in mind that, even though the grade and condition of a card is very important, the player on the card is critical. After all, would you rather have a Mint Gene Green card or a Very Good Sandy Koufax card? Yes, there really was a player named Gene Green. And sure enough, his Topps card was ... green.

For more about cards, see Chapter 2.

FLIPPING

Picking is all about buying items, and then finding buyers for them, so that a nice tidy profit can be made. There are part-time pickers, who possibly are engineers or computer geeks during the day, and then pickers on the weekends and during their other spare time. And then there are full-time pickers, who make their livelihood chasing down treasures. However, even though their intention is to sell everything they find, that doesn't always happen. Sharp pickers also have acquired a shrewd sense of timing, and know when the magic moment has arrived to flip/sell a treasure most profitably.

Sometimes pickers will find an item that they become attached to, and feel that they must keep. There was a baseball picker who went to a yard sale, and found a complete 1962 Topps set. The set was all there in numerical order, Mantle, Koufax, Musial, Colavito, Aaron. They were his heroes. He stood there for a minute thinking about how he went to baseball games with his father and brother when he was a kid. Our picker friend did buy that 1962 card set, and kept it. A similar ending happened with another picker who could not part with a World Series program of a game that he had been to in Los Angeles in 1959.

So these occurrences do happen, even though it is not the intent of the picker. His job is to buy suitable items to flip, not to buy items he will keep.

Pickers are generally knowledgeable about the value of the memorabilia they pick. Pickers will often sell their items in a variety of ways. Sometimes a little trial and error will go a long way.

WHERE PICKERS CAN GO TO FLIP THEIR INVENTORY

- **SPORTS DEALERS.** Most pickers will target their selling efforts to dealers, who are in the best position to buy the items. However, most pickers will establish rapport with dealers ahead of time. Pickers need to be cautious that the dealers are not already saturated with, for example, common cards in average condition. Veteran pickers will have relationships with local, as well as regional and national dealers.
- **TRADE SHOWS.** Many pickers will travel a circuit, and rent booth space at sports shows and conventions. Many cities have monthly sports shows, at which a sports figure will be invited to speak for a few minutes and will also sign autographs. *Sports Collectors Digest* (sportscollectorsdi-

gest.com) and *Beckett Sports Cards Monthly* (beckett.com) magazines are excellent sources of information of upcoming shows. Sometimes pickers will partner with vendors who will be renting space at an upcoming event in case they themselves are not able to attend. Of course, the annual National Sports Collectors Convention draws the most people, but there is more competition to sell items. For more about the convention, visit www.nsccshow.com.

- **ONLINE.** Pickers will often go online to sell their items. This is now a popular picking practice. Many pickers do quite well with selling online, whether it is through eBay or even Craigslist. Just make sure that you take into account the time it will take to ship and package the items.
- **THEIR OWN SALES.** Sometimes pickers will accumulate enough of their own items that they will conduct their own sale. They will have some minimal expense, but their profit may be increased because they will not need to pay a dealer a percentage for selling their items.

NEGOTIATING

The mentality of pickers is: It doesn't hurt to try. If you get turned down, at least I tried. You never know. True enough. Pickers know that there is no harm in asking, so why not?

Pickers also know that some sellers will intentionally set the price of an item higher than what they know it should actually be. Why do they do that? Simple. They know that most pickers will counter the selling price with a price of their own.

As a pickers, you need to determine the lowest price at which you are willing to buy an item. If the verbal battle with a seller reaches the point where the seller wants more than you want to spend, you should walk away.

Haggling is common, and both the picker and seller have come to expect verbal negotiation.

For the picker, it is all part of the journey, the process by which he pursues his goods.

Naturally, there will be some instances when the seller simply will not negotiate. The selling price is the final price, and that is it. No amount of haggling will do any good. At a yard sale, for example, a seller may post signs saying that the prices are set in stone. In that situation, you may still try to negotiate for a lower price. The results may be mixed. In some instances, the seller might not budge an inch. Or, it is quite possible that you may have approached the seller at precisely the right moment, and the seller might be willing to negotiate. It might be the end of the day, and the seller may think that if he or she does not lower the price, then the item will not be sold. Experienced pickers will look for body language cues. But a picker must always remember that if he or she expects to be successful, then any negotiating should be done privately, and not in earshot of other potential buyers.

You may strike it rich. Baseball pickers will have the most success with baseball cards. Why? Because most other baseball items, such as jerseys and signed balls, are commonly sold in auctions. However, some items such as cards, programs, magazines, even books on baseball, are frequently found in garage sales, flea markets, and estate sales. In those situations, the seller may very well have placed a large quantity of, let's say, baseball cards, for sale, and probably did not carefully examine the cards being offered. Most likely the seller did not look to see the condition of the cards, either, and if there were any cards of star players. In fact, the seller may not have even been a baseball fan. Maybe the seller is a woman whose husband is deceased. Maybe the cards were passed down and the seller wanted a quick sale. It is even possible that the seller is moving and wants to get rid of stuff. Sound familiar? Whatever the reason, the picker needs to be prepared to act. What follows are the most profitable tips I can offer:

- **DON'T WASTE YOUR TIME.** If items are clearly marked "non-negotiable," pay heed. Pickers sometimes think that they can negotiate for any item. That is not true. Look for posted signs that all prices are final. But sometimes the seller, such as the person conducting the yard sale for example, may not want to reduce the price, but will do so anyway. Often the seller will deliberately set the price higher to allow for some negotiating. A picker should look around and determine if there will be an opportunity to reduce the price. However, pickers will generally have their best chance to reduce prices when they can communicate directly with the seller.
- **INFORM THE SELLER, IF NECESSARY.** An individual selling

baseball memorabilia may have only a dim—or worse, an exaggerated—view of the value of their items. He might assume that a pennant from the 1950s is valuable based on its age alone. Pickers know that age doesn't necessarily confer value. So it pays, in every sense, to gently probe the seller about price and, when it's appropriate, show an inexperienced seller that his or her prices are out of line.

- **BE COURTEOUS AND POLITE.** The old saying that "you can get more bees with honey than you can with vinegar" definitely holds true. Experienced pickers are aware that if they appear rude or nasty then their chances of being successful will probably diminish. Keep in mind that the seller does not have to reduce the stated price. You are approaching the seller to reduce the price, and certainly being mean or disrespectful will not help your cause. Don't burn bridges. You may need to work with the seller in the future.

- **SCHMOOZE.** It wouldn't hurt to schmooze a little with the seller. Try to build a little rapport. If you are discussing sports items, ask who his favorite team is. Certainly don't argue with him, and if he says that he is rooting for the Red Sox, don't tell him that the Yankees are a better team. Don't bring up sore subjects. If the seller is a Phillies fan, please don't remind him that in 1964 the Phillies blew a 5-1/2 game lead with 8 games to go in the season.

- **SHOW APPRECIATION.** Always remember to raise, not lower, the seller's ego. Compliment the seller on how nice the items for sale are.

- **NEVER CHALLENGE THE SELLER.** Don't offend him by telling him that the Cal Ripken 8 x 10 glossy photo was overpriced and whoever set the price didn't know what he was thinking. That won't get you very far. He may have spent a great deal of time on the sale and you might be catching that person at a bad time. Don't wear out your welcome. Know when to stop talking.

- **HIGHER PRICE = MORE BARGAINING (SOMETIMES).** The more expensive an item is, the more negotiable it is. That's right. The higher the item is being sold for, then probably the higher the seller's profit margin, and the greater chance for the price to be reduced. Of course, a picker needs to keep in mind that the costlier an item to him, then the more he will need to charge to a dealer or elsewhere. It is a vicious circle. Being a picker certainly has its share of risks.

- **BUYER BEWARE**. Examine the items carefully. Pickers don't usually buy an item without really scrutinizing it first. Look for damages of any kind, including scratches, nicks, watermarks, and holes. If you find significant damage to a piece, you may just want to put it down and move on. Or, you may want to show the damage to the seller, and have a heyday reducing the price. Take the case of the picker who saw a Major League Baseball bobbing head doll from the early 1960s being sold for $400. This wasn't any old bobbing head. No, this one was a rare Houston Colt .45s black-faced doll. It can sell for thousands of dollars. The picker thought he had a steal, until the seller removed the tissue around the doll's neck and the picker discovered that the spring was broken. The bobbing head doll had been overpriced, and the picker just passed on it.

- **KNOWLEDGE IS POWER**. Pickers need to know the product. Pickers can't be expected to be knowledgeable about every item, but consider the following: There was a set of Hartland baseball statues that was priced at an estate sale for $1,000. The buyer thought he had made a great purchase, because he figured he could sell it for double his cost. He was familiar with the Hartland set being a favorite among sports collectors. He negotiated the price to $800, and gladly paid. His excitement turned to anger when he did a little research and found out that the set he had purchased was a replica set from the 1980s, not the original set from twenty-five years earlier, and had only a fraction of its value.

- **AVAILABILITY = LEVERAGE**. The more available an item is, the more negotiable it is. Baseball items are rarely one of a kind. There are even several Honus Wagner T206 cards known to exist. Pickers have some leverage with sellers by reminding them that they can purchase the same items elsewhere. For example, a picker may notice a complete set of 2007 Topps baseball cards being sold in a shoebox for $80. The picker knows that he can purchase the same complete set, unopened, for roughly the same price. The experienced picker would kindly tell the seller that he can purchase the 2007 factory set of the same cards for about the same price, and he wouldn't have to go through the shoebox to make sure that all the cards were there.

A picker should know what his options are to obtain the same product. It will greatly enhance his chances of bringing down the price significantly.

- **OFFER CASH.** Money talks. And if you're going to pay by cash, ask for a discount. But remember, once you have paid cash, rather than a check, or credit card, there is little that you can do if you have buyer's remorse.
- **MAKE A REASONABLE OFFER.** Don't lowball the seller so much that it is insulting. You're liable to turn off the seller so much that he or she will simply not want to deal with you.
- **KNOW YOUR LIMIT.** Have an idea what your top dollar figure is for an item before you start negotiating. Don't get carried away at the spur of the moment.
- **HOLD OR FOLD.** Know when to stop talking. Know when to walk away. Know when the negotiations are over.

When possible, negotiate. Prices are sometimes labeled as "invitations to buy, not statements of value." Enjoy the negotiating process, stay calm and collected. Many pickers will profess that it is the journey that counts. Negotiating is certainly part of the picking journey.

SHARING YOUR COLLECTION

Baseball pickers are fans, first and foremost. The game is in our blood. I wouldn't be surprised if someday they find it in our DNA. Many of us grew up collecting baseball cards. I certainly did. I remember marvelous afternoons spent with other boy's trading cards back and forth, and the furious negotiations that ensued: "Wait! I'll give you a Yogi Berra and Elston Howard for that Juan Marichal and Willie McCovey."

Even then, we built our collections by bargaining. Shoeboxes became the repositories of our hopes and dreams for baseball stardom. Cards and other collectibles were our connections to the heroes we idolized. We studied box scores every day to see how our revered White Sox, Royals, Pirates, and any number of other teams were doing. A lot of us, let's face it, still check those statistics every day.

But now we have our own way of keeping score. It's by becoming pickers, which is another way of saying that we have become connoisseurs of the sport we love so much.

And most of us love to share our interest in picking, whether we gather at trade shows or the National Sports Collectors Convention. But we also connect in other ways. The Internet has become a great vehicle for doing that. Websites, such as Collectors Universe (www.collectors.com), are wonderful resources where collectors of all kinds can talk – or even vent – about common topics. It's a great sounding board, as well as a means for meeting and sharing ideas with others.

Likewise, *Sports Collectors Digest* offers collectors an opportunity to talk about their interest in memorabilia. It also provides another marketplace for collectors and pickers to buy and sell.

Collectors of baseball memorabilia almost always offer two standard tips to those new to the activity and I think they're well worth heeding:

First, collect items about players whose skills and personality are important to you, no matter the era. You might be drawn back to Duke Snider, Ernie Banks, or Roger Maris, or to contemporary stars like Miguel Cabrera, Andrew McCutchen, or Joey Votto. Or perhaps you're more inclined to collect items of your favorite team, such as the Seattle Mariners or Arizona Diamondbacks. You might even want to collect by the year or decade. There are many ways to shape a collection and, undoubtedly, approaches that have yet to be tried.

Second, buy quality items. They'll almost always rise in value quicker than more common collectibles, which will make you appreciate them even more as time goes by.

Pickers know that, and their collections of what they choose to keep instead of flip for a profit thrive as a result.

And of course, I have my own tip for you: Enjoy the journey!

Resources

AUCTION COMPANIES

Coach's Corner Sports Auctions
www.myccsa.com
47 N. Front St.
Souderton, PA 18964
215-721-9162
email: contact@myccsa.com

Goodwin & Co.
www.goodwinandco.com
9607 Mill Hill Lane
St. Louis, MO 63127
314-849-9798
email: bill@goodwinandco.com

Heritage Auctions
www. ha.com
3500 Maple Ave.
Dallas, TX 75219.3941
877-437-4824
email: Bid@ha.com

Inside the Park Collectibles
insidetheparkcollectibles.com
10 Churchill Dr.
New Hyde Park, NY 11040
516-747-7932
email: Sharlou28@aol.com

Lelands
www.lelands.com
12 American Way, #8
South Dennis, MA 02660
516-409-9700
email: info@lelands.com

Robert Edward Auctions
www.robertedwardauctions.com
PO Box 7256
Watchung, NJ 07069
908-226-9900
email: info@
robertedwardauctions.com

Sports Collectors, LTD.
8135 Elizabeth Ave.
Orland Park IL 60462
708-873-1195

CARD-GRADING SERVICES

Beckett Grading Services
www.beckett.com
4635 McEwen Road
Dallas, TX 75244
972-991-6657

Professional Sports Authenticator
www.psacard.com
PSA, Professional Sports
Authenticator
P.O. Box 6180
Newport Beach, CA 92658
800-325-1121
email: info@psacard.com

Sportscard Guaranty LLC
www.sgccard.com
8-E Easy Street, Suite 1
Bound Brook NJ 08805
800-SGC-9212 or 973-984-0018

Index

About the Author

Jeff Figler is one of the world's leading experts on sports, presidential, and pop culture collectibles. He is the author of *Collecting for Beginners and Collectible Wisdom*, and has written for the *San Diego Union-Tribune*, and the *St. Louis Post-Dispatch, StL Today, Sports Collectors Digest*, and several magazines in the collectibles field. He is also a popular speaker on cruise ships.

Jeff is the director of Jeff Figler's Sports Appraisals, Ltd., and can be reached at collectingwithjeff@sbcglobal.net.

Jeff and his wife, Linda, live in San Diego, St. Louis, and Bearsted, England.

TOP COLLECTOR GUIDES FOR ANY HOBBYIST

KrauseBooks.com is your one-stop shop for all of your hobby and collecting needs. Whether you are just getting started or have been collecting for years, our products will help you build, identify, appraise and maintain your collections.

You'll find great products at great prices throughout the site and we even offer FREE Shipping on purchases over $49.

Be sure to sign up for to receive exclusive offers and discounts!

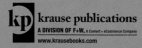